From the *Cross* to the *Church*

The Emergence of the Church from the Chaos of the Crucifixion

A. C. Graziano

WestBow
PRESS
A DIVISION OF THOMAS NELSON

WestBow Press books may be ordered through booksellers or by contacting:

WestBow Press
A Division of Thomas Nelson
1663 Liberty Drive
Bloomington, IN 47403
www.westbowpress.com
1-(866) 928-1240

Because of the dynamic nature of the Internet, any web addresses or links contained in
this book may have changed since publication and may no longer be valid. The views
expressed in this work are solely those of the author and do not necessarily reflect the
views of the publisher, and the publisher hereby disclaims any responsibility for them.

Any people depicted in stock imagery provided by Thinkstock are models,
and such images are being used for illustrative purposes only.

Certain stock imagery © Thinkstock.

ISBN: 978-1-4497-9897-0 (sc)
ISBN: 978-1-4497-9898-7 (hc)
ISBN: 978-1-4497-9896-3 (e)

Library of Congress Control Number: 2013911276

Printed in the United States of America.

WestBow Press rev. date: 5/9/2014

Table of Contents

Introduction

The first documents we have from the Christian era are the epistles of Paul, dating from the early fifties to the early sixties. Wouldn't you like to know what happened before those first documents were written? If Jesus died in or near the year 30, what did his followers say and do in the next 5 years, the next 20 years, the next 30 years, before the first gospel was written?

Some very great minds have tried to answer these questions. The tools used by these scholars include several specific forms of exegesis which will be explained in plain, clear language.

We start with the gospel of Paul. Paul, as you know, did not write a gospel. Paul preached a gospel, the "good news" (gospel) that God offers salvation to all who believe in Jesus, his son. We shall see how scholars are trying to recover the original texts of the written gospels and how they explain the formation of the gospels.

Sure to be surprising are the various forms of Christianity in the first century of the Christian era. Some were ancestors of the orthodox catholic church, some were enthusiastic believers, many were groups who punished their bodies (ascetic, some even extremely ascetic), some were orgiastic, some elite, some monarchical. We know that orthodoxy won out, mostly, but how, why, when?

The works produced by these scholars are sometimes easy to read, sometimes nearly impenetrable, and sometimes boring. That's why we compiled this work, to make their ideas, the fruits of lifetimes of work by many scholars, available to ordinary readers who are interested in the emergence of Christianity.

Enjoy.

Chapter One: Jesus was a Jew

Our understanding of Jesus must be conditioned through the prism of his Jewishness. All of us know what a Jew is. Our knowledge comes from personal relationships and from the first five books of the bible, the books of Moses, also called the Pentateuch, also called the Torah or Law. What if Moses did not write the Pentateuch? What if much of the material in those books may be understood best as a foundation myth, a created remembrance explaining why we are doing something today when the reason for doing it has long ago receded into the fog of times forgotten? Is it possible that the Judaism we have experienced in our lifetime is, like the Christianity we have experienced in our lifetime, milk toast, thin gruel standing in for a richer diversity in former times? Chances are, even if we are or know Jews very well, we do not know Judaism very well. It is easier for us lazy humans to repeat a mantra, a creed or a stereotype than to think about it. This definitely misses the mark when thinking about Judaism. The genius of Judaism—its ability to adapt to changing circumstances—is rivaled only by that of its elder daughter, Christianity.

A Stark Summary of the Biblical Narrative, What We Were Taught

In the Pentateuch, we read of Abram or Abraham leaving the land of Ur to travel to Egypt, and then to Canaan, today's Palestine. Yahweh, the personal name of a particular god, visits Abraham for a meal. Before that, however, Yahweh made a covenant with Abraham: Yahweh

1

promised to give Canaan to Abraham and his descendents in perpetuity; the sign of the covenant is circumcision of all males, whether native born or purchased. This is a unique feature of the Jewish religion: it is a religion of contract (covenant) with each party obliged to do something.

Yahweh allows Abraham's ancient, barren wife Sara to bear a child, Isaac. There is the famous story of the sacrifice of Isaac by Abraham, averted at the last minute by Yahweh. Years later, Yahweh wrestles with Jacob, Abraham's grandson. Jacob (also called Israel) becomes Abraham's heir because Esau, his older brother, sold his birthright to Jacob for a plate of beans.

Israel (Jacob) has twelve sons. These families grow to become the twelve tribes of Israel. Israel favored his eleventh son, Joseph, which caused his brothers to envy him. The eleven of the twelve conspire against Joseph, and Joseph is sold into slavery in Egypt. Joseph rises to a position of power in Egypt. Meanwhile, famine strikes Canaan and his brothers go to Egypt in search of food. Joseph, without rancor, saves his brothers, the eleven conspirators.

Their descendents become enslaved by the Egyptians, but, led by Moses, escape from Egypt. The army of six hundred thousand men, along with their families, wandered in the desert for forty years on the way to the promised land, Canaan. Moses sees Canaan from afar, but it is Joshua who conquers Canaan for the returning Israelites.

The twelve tribes are finally united into a kingdom first by Saul, a military hero. David, of Goliath fame, became the next king, founding the Davidic dynasty. David's son, Solomon, extends the kingdom and builds the Temple, the dwelling place of Yahweh. Yahweh, like other gods of other nations, dwells in the Temple's Holy of Holies.

The Kingdom breaks up into a northern kingdom, Samaria, and a southern kingdom, Judea. Samaria is conquered by the Assyrians in 723 BCE or thereabouts, and Judea is conquered by the Babylonians in 587 or thereabouts.

An Alternative Explanation

The authorship of the Torah by Moses was virtually unchallenged until the seventeenth century. Today, modern scholars accept as fact that the Pentateuch has several sources and was fashioned by an unknown number of redactors (a compiler or editor). More on that in chapter nine.

The advances in biblical research come not only from textual analysis, but also from archaeology. What follows is an alternative explanation of the origin of the Jews based on textual study, analysis of well-dated historical documents outside the bible, and archaeology.

Before the Exodus

Egyptian records are silent on the subject of Israelites except for an inscription on the Merneptah Stele[1] dated 1206 BCE, which celebrates a victory over Israel. "Israel has been shorn. Its seed no longer exists."

It is thought that the ruins of the city of Pi-Ramesse near present day Tanis represent a city described in the bible as built by Hebrews. Ramesses II is the most frequently cited Pharaoh under whom the exodus took place. If, in fact, he is the ruler at the time of the exodus, then the date of the exodus lies between Ramesses II, 1,279 BCE and the Merneptah stele, 1,208 BCE. Keep in mind that the stele celebrates victory over the people known as Israel in the land of Canaan.

Archaeology and extra-biblical sources describe thirteenth century BCE Canaan as a number of fortified city-states, each with its own ruler. Virtually all were tributaries to Egypt. There were definite economic class distinctions. Better off Canaanites enjoyed large houses and imported decorated pottery. In a period of economic decline, heavy tribute demands imposed by Egypt were in part paid by high taxes and in part by enslaving the poorest Canaanites to Egypt.

The straightened economy was accompanied by an increase in the number of settlements in the hill country which cannot be explained by natural growth. Most villages are small, perhaps home to one hundred people. The houses are simple and similar to one another through

---

1   Merneptah: Egyptian Pharaoh, son of Ramesses the Great. Stele: an upright slab bearing sculptured designs or inscriptions.

villages. The earliest villages reflected a more pastoral way of life, leading to greater reliance on farming. Pottery was simple and unadorned. The villages lacked large residences or monumental architecture of any kind. We know nothing of their burial customs. The inhabitants were very likely polytheistic idolaters. These Israelite villages are farming villages built on bedrock soil with most showing no evidence of conflict.

The contrast between Canaanite city-states and Israeli villages coupled with the explosion of the number of villages has lead some scholars to suggest that poorer Canaanites revolted or fled to the hill country, where they established a subsistence living in virtual economic equality—everybody is poor.

Excavations in the 1930's produced evidence of the destruction of Jericho, but that destruction is now dated to about 1,500 BCE. Joshua is also credited with the destruction of Ai, but Ai was destroyed around 2,200 BCE. Hazor, destroyed around 1,250 BCE is being excavated now. According to Amnon Ben-Tor, the archeologist in charge of the excavation, the city was conquered by the Israelites. Sharon Zuckerman, also working on the excavation, believes the city could have been destroyed by revolution. Of the thirty-one sites the Torah lists as conquered by Joshua, few showed any signs of war.

Consider the following three suppositions. First, economic decline and perhaps other factors lead to the disintegration or destruction of the city-states of Canaan during the thirteenth century BCE. Second, revolt, flight, or both revolt and flight of poor Canaanites lead to the foundation of hundreds of villages in the hill country. Third, the conquest of Canaan by Joshua is a theological construct, a composition created to help explain, along with the stories of the Patriarchs, the origin of the Israelites. If these suppositions are accurate, then the Israelites are in origin polytheistic Canaanites. They were not outsiders conquering polytheistic Canaanites. This would help explain the idol worship of the Jews throughout the date range of Hebrew Bible writings.[2]

---

2   This picture, relying in part on *The Bible's Buried Secrets* (see Sources), is fundamentally confirmed in Finklestein & Silberman's work, *The Bible Unearthed* (see Sources). Our reading of their work suggests that reading the first eight or so books of the Hebrew Bible as religious documents may be incorrect. They posit composition of most of these works in seventh century Judea, where political

Key Points

- The biblical narrative explaining the origin of the Jews is highly poetic. There is little archeological evidence to support its accounts until approximately the tenth century BCE. Likewise, extra-biblical evidence before that time is lacking except for the Merneptah Stele, which describes an Egyptian victory over the Israelites, not Canaanites, in Canaan at the end of the thirteenth century BCE.
- There is a dramatic change in Canaan. The palaces of the rich in the city-states decline, and poor Canaanites revolt or flee to the hill country to establish farming villages.
- Of the thirty-one sites which the Torah lists as conquered by Joshua, few showed any signs of war. Of three cities supposedly conquered by Joshua, two were clearly outside the probable period of Joshua's activity.
- The combination of the decline of Canaanite city-states, along with the likelihood that the sweeping conquest of Canaan by Joshua is a theological construct, lead to the conclusion that the original Israeli villages were founded and peopled by Canaanites. This is to say that polytheistic Canaanites are the people who became known as Israelites, and later as Jews.

The Exodus Narrative

As you might expect, scholars differ in dating the origins of the written Torah. In presenting one alternative here, with some possible variations, keep in mind there are other theories.

A primitive Hebrew alphabet (abecedary) dating to the tenth century BCE was discovered at Tel Zayit, at the edge of David's kingdom. Its discovery in a remote area is cited as evidence that literacy was

---

objectives may have been paramount. If our understanding is correct, it is simply another example of the use of religion in statecraft by autocratic governments.

widespread, having reached a relatively unimportant frontier town. Widespread literacy does not necessarily mean that many people could read and write; it just means that in just about any place one or more could read and write. This discovery argues for the early writing of biblical accounts.

Scholars see the oldest Hebrew, based on changes over time in grammar, script, and the meanings of words, in the Hebrew Bible Book of Exodus. Also, the exodus is the event most often mentioned in the Hebrew Bible. Parts of Exodus, like 15: 4, which has been characterized as the "Song of the Sea," are thought to have existed as poetry before the invention of writing.

The exodus described in Exodus involved six hundred thousand men plus their families.[3] They took forty years to get to Canaan. Yet, despite a hundred years of archeological diggings, there is no archeological evidence of such a mass movement.

On the other hand, not only is the exodus the most frequently mentioned event in the Hebrew Bible, there are elements of the exodus in all four principal sources of the Torah. The importance of the exodus to later Israelites cannot be ignored.

In the first book of the Pentateuch, Genesis, there are the legends of the Patriarchs, Abraham, Isaac and Jacob, the last of whom is also called Israel. Legends? There may have been some very early oral traditions, but the closest stories to those in Genesis which have been found are of Mesopotamian provenance. It is likely that if there were any early traditions, those traditions would have been formulated from these sources and circulated like the telling of the *Iliad*. The numbers and ages in Genesis are so incredible that some scholars doubt even the existence of Abraham. Also, some Genesis accounts use the personal name of God, Yahweh. Most scholars date this source to no earlier than the tenth century BCE, and some date it hundreds of years later. If the name of God has been retrojected into the stories of the Patriarchs, covenant and circumcision may also have been retrojected to form a

---

3   Exodus 12: 37. All translations of the Hebrew Bible and the New Testament are taken from the English Standard Version of the Holy Bible unless otherwise noted. *The Holy Bible, English Standard Version*. (Crossway; Wheaton, Ill, 2001). Some of the discussion of the Exodus depends upon *The Bible's Buried Secrets* (see Sources).

theological construct to make the survivors of the exodus the heirs of Yahweh's promise to Abraham.

The second book, Exodus, describes the marvelous departure of the Israelites—they technically are not Jews yet since there is no Law—from Egypt. The first book of the Hebrew Bible after the Pentateuch, Joshua, tells the story of the magnificent military campaign which secured the land of Canaan for the Israelites. In these books we have narratives describing the Israelites as outsiders, coming to the Promised Land as Yahweh's Chosen People. Why?

One possible explanation is that at the time these traditions came to be written down, probably in the sixth century BCE, the redactors were profoundly embarrassed by their polytheistic origins. They saw the Babylonian Captivity as Yahweh's punishment for their practice of idolatry. Thus, the history they were writing must eradicate completely this tradition of polytheism and swear allegiance to Yahweh only. The priestly redactors hated the idolatry of the people of Canaan and defined themselves as a people totally different from the Canaanites. But this occurred centuries later, when the Pentateuch was becoming a document.

What about the exodus, that supremely important event? The exodus becomes a supremely important event because it fits the theological narrative of the redactors who were responsible for the compilation of the Pentateuch. The Israelis, fleeing from Egypt, were about to wrest the promised land, Canaan, from the hands of idolatrous Canaanites. Now there was a whole cloth: a covenant promise by Yahweh and circumcision acceptance by the chosen people; the descent of the Israelites from the Patriarchs; the chosen people of Yahweh flee oppression in Egypt with the mighty help of Yahweh; the Israelites claim their right to Canaan according to Yahweh's promise to Abraham; to prove their otherness from the Canaanites, Yahweh orders the Israelites to exterminate the Canaanites. Was there a basis in fact for the exodus narrative? Very likely.

The Canaanite rulers shipped poor Canaanites to Egypt as slaves in partial payment of tribute to the Pharaoh. At some point in the thirteenth century BCE, a group of these, probably small in number and certainly not six hundred thousand men plus their families, escaped. Perhaps there were several escapes at different times. As to the details of the account in Exodus, each must be considered on its own merits. We shall consider only one, the burning bush (Exodus 3: 1-15).

Moses was tending the flock of his father-in-law Jethro in Midian when he sees the burning bush which is not consumed. In his conversation with Yahweh, Yahweh tells Moses his name and establishes that he is the God of Abraham, Isaac and Jacob (Israel). This epiphany somehow ties the Patriarchs, who could not have been Jews since there was no Law in their lifetimes, to the Jews, as the inheritors of the promises Yahweh made to Abraham.

In Midian lived a people called the Shasu. They lived in a town called YHW.[4] If the town reflected the name of the local god, the name Yahweh perhaps is discovered, although not its pronunciation or its meaning. If the Shasu were helpful to the runaway slaves, it would have been natural for the runaways to adopt their god, along with their other gods, of course.

Some of the refugees may have had long-ago contacts, neighbors, even relatives, with the villagers in the hill country of Canaan. When the runaways reach these Israelite villages, they likely would have been welcomed to some degree as oppressed people, and their tales about the good god Yahweh, who helped them escape the Pharaoh, would prompt the Canaanite Israelites to add Yahweh to their pantheon. As time goes by, the nature of Yahweh's assistance is enhanced, and when the Pentateuch comes to be written some five to six hundred years later, in exile and humiliation for their polytheistic past, the entire enterprise makes sense to the redactors. A grand plan of covenant, promise and protection becomes evident. Yahweh is retrojected into the patriarchal legends, Abraham becomes the father of the "chosen people" who escape from Egypt with marvelous assistance from Yahweh, and, as outsiders, conquer Canaan, slaying its polytheistic natives.

If we think about the Boston Massacre or "the shot heard 'round the world," we can see how important events in a nation's history take on mythic proportions even in a modern, literate society. A group

---

4   Ancient written Hebrew had no vowel signs. The personal name of God, Yahweh, would have been rendered (in our script) as YHWH. The Hebrew letters composing this word are called the tetragrammaton. As an aside, the conjunction of the vowels of the Hebrew word *Adonai* with the tetragrammaton yielded Jehovah, a thoroughly unscriptural word.

escape from slavery over three thousand years ago in an ancient society where miracles and multiple gods controlled the fates of both the individuals and the group would be remembered, celebrated, and finally mythologized in the telling and retelling of the story.

To see the extent to which this can happen, consider the stories surrounding Moses. He is abandoned to die as an infant but is rescued and brought up as the Pharaoh's daughter's son. Then he kills an Egyptian in righteous anger and flees to Midian. After he tends the sheep of his father-in-law, he returns to Egypt, negotiates with the Pharaoh of Egypt and performs miracles. He acts as the prophet (mouthpiece) of Yahweh, as a lawgiver, and as a military commander. He presides over sacrifices, and, in writing the Pentateuch, documents the history of the Jews. Moses develops the cult of the Temple, and organizes a priesthood. The ark of the covenant, the dwelling place of Yahweh, is his design. It is clearly possible that the historical Moses was less talented than the Moses of the Pentateuch.

Key Points

- The exodus is the most frequently mentioned event in the Hebrew Bible. There are elements of the exodus in all four principal sources of the Torah. The importance of the exodus to later Israelites cannot be ignored.
- The biblical characterization of the exodus as the movement of six hundred thousand men plus their families over a period of forty years is very likely the sort of mythological exaggeration found elsewhere in the Pentateuch. A very much smaller slave escape or series of escapes from Egypt is more credible.
- It is possible, but hardly certain, that the escaped slaves adopted Yahweh into their pantheon on the way to Canaan.
- If so, it is quite possible that their hosts, or fellow runaways, in Canaan, who may have been political refugees from oppressive overlords, added to their polytheistic pantheon the good god Yahweh, the rescuer of the escaped slaves.

- When, during and after the Babylonian Captivity, these events were historicized, they were conflated along with the Patriarchal legends into a theological construct (a foundation myth in this case) to deny their polytheistic origins and to avoid the guilt of idol worship, the sin which caused Yahweh to permit the Babylonian Captivity.

Did Yahweh Have a Wife?

El was the principal deity in the Canaanite pantheon. Throughout Israeli villages there have been found thousands of figurines of a bull, which is understood to be a representation of El. Also found in the thousands are little statues of Asherah, the mother goddess or fertility goddess of the Canaanites. There are no known representations of Yahweh, and it is easy to assume that Asherah was a consort of El. However, inscriptions linking Asherah to Yahweh have been discovered. Furthermore, 2 Kings 23 describes the reforms of King Josiah (second half of the seventh century BCE). Among these reforms are destroying Temple vessels made for Baal, Asherah, and "for all the host of heaven." He ordered to be destroyed the Temple Asherah (a pole sacred to or representing Asherah) and the sanctuaries where idol cults existed outside the Temple. "And he broke down the houses of the male cult prostitutes who were in the house of the Lord, where the women wove hangings for the Asherah."[5]

Key Points

- The exodus is a fulcrum event in Jewish identity. But the biblical account assumes Jewish identity before there were Jews, that is, in the age of the Patriarchs, before

---

5   2 Kings 23: 7. As a fertility goddess, common people found Asherah necessary for good crops and the birth of sons. She is often represented as a pole or tree, sometimes as a grove of trees. Folk religion differed from the Jerusalem cult probably as a rule before the Exile and almost continuously afterwards as well, just as today many people pick and choose which elements of their religions to which they must adhere.

Yahweh gave to Moses the Law. Furthermore, there is an absence of archeological confirmation of a mass movement—six hundred thousand men plus their dependents—over a period of forty years.

- The economic degradation of Canaanite city-states may have resulted in poorer Canaanites being shipped to Egypt in payment of tribute, and the flight of poorer Canaanites to the hill country to escape their Canaanite overlords.
- A relatively small group of Canaanite slaves escaping from Egypt may provide the historical kernel of the mass movement recited in Exodus. The conflation of the historical event would not be unusual—almost expected—in the traditions of oral transmission.
- On their way to Canaan, the escaped slaves may have run into and adopted Yahweh into their pantheon.
- The Canaanite hill country villagers could appreciate the quest for freedom by runaway slaves, perhaps their former neighbors, even relatives. It would have been easy to add Yahweh to their pantheon based on the wonderful assistance he provided to the runaways.
- The "Israelites" now have an identity: a polytheistic people living in small, separate villages who are largely Canaanite in origin.

The Kingdom of Israel

After several centuries, the families in the villages have grown into tribes. Disunited, they are harassed by the "Sea People," probably, at least in some cases, mercenaries hired by Egypt to subdue the area and secure tribute. One group, the Philistines, proved to be especially troublesome because of their iron age technology. This outward threat compels the tribes to unite and sets the stage for the united Kingdom of Israel, with Saul, David, and Solomon as the first and only kings of the united kingdom. (Rehoboam, Solomon's son and successor, briefly reigned over the united kingdom, but the kingdom split into two during his reign.)

By the tenth century BCE we have archeological evidence which supports various biblical accounts of the Kingdom. Excavations in Jerusalem have uncovered what may be a wall from the Palace of David. Excavations have discovered identical six chamber gates in Hazor, Megiddo and Gezer, as described in I Kings 9: 15. Pharaoh Shishak raided Israel in 925, five years after Solomon's death in 930 (2 Chronicles 12: 2). He bragged about carrying off the treasures of the Temple and the Palace and destroying the gate at Gezer. Clearly, the gate at Gezer, and very likely the similar gates at Hazor and Megiddo, were built during the reign of Solomon, implying a forceful and somewhat prosperous central authority.[6] Finally, the discovery of a stele at Tel Dan (dated to 840 BCE) provides archeological evidence of the House of David.

Except for the reforms of King Josiah, both the bible and archeological evidence—thousands of figurines—support the notion of a polytheistic pre-exilic Israel. Not only were the folks in the hinterlands not under the rule of Temple worship, but, as acknowledged in the bible itself, the idols sometimes made their way into the Temple worship.

The united Kingdom of Israel did not survive Solomon's successor, Rehoboam. The ten tribes living in the north of the kingdom established the Kingdom of Israel about 930 BCE. It lasted about two hundred years until it was overrun by the Assyrians. The Assyrians carried off much of the population and encouraged Assyrians and others to settle in this area (Samaria). The population became a mixed population and was shunned by the Jews in the southern kingdom.

The southern Kingdom of Judah persisted until about 587 BCE when it was overrun by the Babylonians. At least the royal family and the priests were carried to Babylonia, the priests taking with them their writings and oral traditions.

The Babylonian Captivity was both remarkable and terrible. It was terrible to the Jews because they had lost the Temple, the dwelling place of Yahweh and the heart of their professed religious identity. They had lost their royal family and their High Priest. They had lost their land. There was nothing left. This result constituted pure evil. Why did this happen?

---

6   Actually, Finkelstein and Silberman (*The Bible Unearthed*) disagree emphatically with this dating, placing the gates some 200 years later. They contend the biblical account was written in the reign of Josiah (7th c BCE) and revised again later.

The Babylonian Captivity was remarkable in that the Jews, unlike virtually all other conquered peoples, did not desert their god and adopt the gods of their conquerors, who are clearly the more powerful gods. Instead, reflecting upon their experience, they solved the problem of evil—how can a just person suffer evil in a world ruled by a beneficent and just god?—by blaming themselves: Yahweh was faithful to his promises; the Jews were not faithful. Yahweh justly punished the Jews for their infidelity.[7] The only way to peace was strict obedience to Yahweh.

The ruminations of the priests led them to redact their written and oral traditions into the Pentateuch we have today, more or less. The Patriarchs become the fathers of the chosen people. Yahweh promises Canaan to them in return for faithful service, signed by their acceptance of circumcision. The chosen people escape from slavery in Egypt and conquer Canaan, slaying, as required by Yahweh, all of its idolatrous inhabitants.

Yahweh is supremely faithful. It is his chosen people who are unfaithful and deserving of punishment. The only way to avoid the just punishments of Yahweh is to abide by his law, first and especially by extirpating idolatry and polytheism. The remaining task is to abide by the Torah by the most careful and rigorous interpretation of the Law and traditions surrounding the Law. The precepts of the Law are then elaborated by oral tradition into very detailed rules, which eventually become written rules in the Babylonian and Palestinian Talmuds.

The stories of the Patriarchs are developed to include encounters between the Patriarchs and Yahweh. Whatever their sources, the Patriarchs are linked to the Law by claiming that Israel originated with the Patriarchs, and, therefore, Israel is the rightful heir to the promises Yahweh made to Abraham. To secure this point, it is quite possible that ritual circumcision is retrojected into the Patriarchal narratives. It is worth noting that Israel alone among the nations expresses its relationship to the deity as a contract (covenant), the signing thereto was circumcision. (Yahweh does not sign: he promises.)

---

7   This is not a wholly satisfactory solution to the problem of evil in that the punishments of Yahweh are distributed collectively, such that the just person in the nation suffers evil simply because she is a member of the group.

Now we have a foundation myth. The need is to explain the origin of the Israelites. But, there are restrictions. The polytheistic Canaanites must be seen as enemies of the Jews and destroyed, since their idolatry—actually the idolatry of the Israelites—caused Yahweh to permit the Babylonian captivity of the Jews in Judea. Yet, the land of Canaan must be promised to the Jews by covenant with Yahweh. This is accomplished by retrojecting Yahweh and circumcision into the mythological Patriarchical stories, arriving at a covenant which promises Canaan to the Jews in perpetuity. This is not to say that there are no oral predecessors of the Patriarchal narratives, for there probably were. This is simply an attempt to explain how these traditions were used to explain the origin of the Israelites. From these rose modern Judaism.

<u>Key Points</u>

- In the last part of the eleventh century BCE, Israelite communities find it necessary to unite in order to fight aggression. Saul, David, and Solomon are the first three rulers of the united kingdom.
- The united kingdom lasts about one hundred years before splitting into two kingdoms.
- The Kingdom of Israel, the northern kingdom, is destroyed by the Assyrians in the latter part of the eighth century BCE. Assyrians and others settle there. The population becomes mixed, and, in spite of attempts by the Samaritans to keep a Temple ritual, the inhabitants of the southern kingdom shun Samaritans and a great enmity grows between the peoples.
- The Kingdom of Judea is overrun by the Babylonians in the early part of the sixth century BCE. The ruling classes, and perhaps others, are carried off to Babylonia in exile.
- Unlike most defeated nations, the Jews did not adopt the gods of their conquerors. Instead, they clung to their Yahweh tradition and developed an explanation for the problem of evil.

- In exile, the priestly class redacts documents and oral traditions to produce the Pentateuch we know today, more or less. It establishes the origin of Israel with Abraham, Isaac, and Jacob (Israel), and faithful devotion to Yahweh from time immemorial up to the present day, a theological construct.

Further Development over Time

Scholars agree that the exile is a major moment in the formation of Judaism, although there is some disagreement on the details. Even before the exile, there are Israelites living in places other than Palestine, but these could look fondly back to their homeland. With the exile, there is no homeland; the Israelites in Samaria are rejected and despised; the captives in Babylonia try to explain their woeful misfortune; even the Jews remaining in Judea have lost the Temple, its priests, and their leaders.

Obviously, a great adjustment is required. Jews must learn to be faithful to Yahweh apart from the Temple, apart from homeland, apart from priesthood, apart from the House of David, apart from all the institutions which had previously characterized their Jewishness. Over time, the Temple is replaced by the synagogue, animal sacrifice is replaced by prayers (public prayers, perhaps, began around this time), priests yield to sages (Pharisees, Scribes) and eventually to rabbis, and prophecy ends. Sabbath observance and exclusiveness (circumcision, prohibition on intermarriage, monotheism) become elaborated requirements, the new hallmarks of Jewishness. This allows Jews to exist as Jews in any land. As long as they are Jews according to the Law, where they live is their homeland. This is a remarkable achievement: survival through adaptation.

<u>Key Points</u>

- From the exile, the Jews give the world the idea of a single, spiritual, all-powerful God, who shall have no other gods before him.
- He, alone, is the creator and sustainer of the world.

- This single spiritual God is so apart in holiness that he would forever be unknown by us unless he had chosen to reveal himself through sacred scripture.
- God will reward good and punish evil in the life after death.
- Early Judaism did not survive the exile. Its history was rewritten to facilitate its survival, through stages, into modern Judaism.

The Hellenization of Jewish Thought

Angels arrive in Jewish thought as a gift of the Babylonian Exile.

In another development, the conquests of Alexander the Great brought Greek language and thought to the Jews. Through the process of Hellenization, there arises, among the lower classes, especially the Pharisees, a belief in the existence of the soul, and life after death, new concepts to Judaism. The notion of reward and punishment in the hereafter eventually replaces the previous definitive belief that Yahweh rewards good and punishes evil in this present life.

Some Hellenization would have occurred simply by cultural osmosis. The theological developments mentioned above may well fit that pattern. The Jews were permitted by their Seleucid overlord, the ruler of modern day Syria, to practice their religion without interference from the overlord. (This was a common concession to defeated people, to promote stability.)

Some Jews, however, especially the upper classes, saw positive values in Hellenic culture. The High Priest Jason (175-171 BCE) promoted Greek values, and his successor, Menelaus went so far as to introduce foreign gods into the Temple.

The extreme behavior of Menelaus, especially his plunder of the Temple treasury, provoked violent opposition. In order to quell this rioting, the Seleucid King, Antiochus IV Epiphanes, the overlord of Palestine, entered Jerusalem (167 BCE), slaughtering many of its inhabitants. He introduced idol worship and cultic prostitution into the Temple and forbade circumcision, observance of the Sabbath and other festivals on pain of death.

These outrages provoked the Maccabean revolt (166-160 BCE), which ultimately founded the Hasmonean dynasty (164-63 BCE). The Hasmoneans worked to reduce Greek influence, to re-assert traditional cult, and to eliminate paganism. An internal dispute led to the conquest of Palestine by Rome in 63 BCE.

Key Points

- The spread of Greek thought and culture abetted the development of Jewish thought to include the notion of the soul and belief in reward and punishment after death.
- The positive values of Hellenic culture appealed to the upper classes who promoted Hellenization to such extremes that violence erupted in Jerusalem.
- The Seleucid ruler withdrew permission to practice Jewish religion undisturbed and, instead, essentially forbade the practice of Judaism.
- The Maccabean revolt resulted in the re-establishment of Judaism under the Hasmonean dynasty, which lasted until 63 BCE.

Judaism at the time of Jesus

At the time of Jesus, Judea was a Roman province. In general, the Romans relied upon the Jews to collect taxes and handle routine judicial functions. The Jewish governing power was shared by the High Priest and the Sanhedrin, a council of significant persons.

The Sanhedrin would contain Sadducees, the relatively wealthy priestly aristocracy, and perhaps Scribes, quasi-lawyers. These upper classes tended to be conservative in religion. They would have insisted that the written Law alone was the rule of faith. They would have rejected the Hellenistic notion of reward or punishment after death and the Pharisaic notion that the Law needed to be defined further by oral tradition.

The Sanhedrin would probably not have contained Pharisees, those middle class or lower middle class teachers who believed that oral tradition was as important as the written Law, and who, around this time, forbade the writing down of oral tradition. They were coming to the position that the oral law was given to Moses on Mt. Sinai (as the Roman Catholic Church would later find the bodily assumption of Mary and the infallibility of the Pope in the gospels it deemed canonical). This is the class of teachers who would eventually morph into rabbis and, over the course of six or more centuries, redact a definitive version of the Hebrew bible, write the Babylonian Talmud and the Jerusalem or Palestinian Talmud, and develop a vowel system for pronouncing Hebrew.

It is unlikely that the Sanhedrin had Zealots as members, those Jews who were determined to cast off Roman (or any other foreign influence) and to defend Jewish independence. It may have contained some Herodians, supporters of Herod Antipas who accepted his position as a client of Rome. The Essenes, those followers of the Teacher of Light, had as little as possible to do with the Jerusalem crowd and the Temple rite, and clearly would not sit with the Sanhedrin even if they had been invited.

<u>Key Points</u>

- Several Jewish religious opinions obtained at the time of Christ. There are at least three major factions, the Sadducees, the Pharisees, and the Essenes with a wide variety of gradations within each group.
- The religious mix would shortly become more complicated when the Christians, in the form of Nazarenes, Ebionites, and others developed as sects of Judaism.
- Judaism was not politically united at the time of Christ. The Zealots condemned the Herodians and the power structure in general, and that feeling was mutual. The last thing the latter wanted was war, devastation and greater Roman control.
- Over the next six centuries, this rich mix would devolve into pharisaic-rabbinic Judaism. The Sadducees would

disappear along with the priesthood and the Temple cult, as would the Essenes. The Herodians and Zealots would be crushed by Rome. The Scribes would secularize or be caught in the pharisaic-rabbinic orbit.

- The Christian churches would, by the fourth century CE, be condemned (Ebionites) or overwhelmed (Nazarenes, Cerenthians, and others) by the Christianity Paul had founded.
- Both rabbinic Judaism and orthodox Christianity would attempt to re-write their histories to make it appear that from the very beginning their versions of their religions had always been the one true story and that all others were heterodox.[8]

---

8   See John Dominic Crossan's *The Birth of Christianity* (see Sources).

Chapter Two: Paul was a Jew

What was it like at the crucifixion of Jesus? Mark, and Matthew, following Mark, report that there were women watching from a distance. Luke is silent on witnesses. John places John the Apostle, who could have founded a school of thought and preaching which ultimately produced the *Gospel according to John*, near the cross in a touching scene in which Jesus commends his mother and John to each other.

Surely, this was the end. Not even his closest followers stood by, no doubt in fear of their lives. The person whom Peter declared to be the Christ, the Son of the living God, is nailed to a gibbet, and Peter himself seeks safety away.[9]

But we know it was not the end. It was the beginning. How did the strong and vigorous Church of Christ arise from this morass of defeat and gloom? We begin with the earliest writings accepted as New Testament scripture, the epistles of Paul.

The Gospel of Paul

Perhaps the shortest, simplest expression of the gospel of Paul is found in Romans 10: 9. "…because if you confess with your mouth that Jesus is Lord and believe in your heart that God raised him from the dead, you will be saved."

What could be simpler or more direct? Yet, theologians have fought for two thousand years over the place of works—good deeds—as opposed

---

9   Matthew: 16: 16.

to faith alone in the plan of salvation. The great Lutheran theologian, Karl Barth, following St. Augustine, seems to have forged an unwilling consensus about the sole necessity of faith, but his opponents are reluctant to give up entirely the notion that righteous living—deeds—is also required for salvation. Indeed, one could cite many passages from Paul's epistles which promote his conceptions of righteousness, avoidance of uncleanliness and love of neighbor. But much of his advice makes little sense to modern readers. Did it make sense to his listeners?

It may or may not be obvious that what was righteous in the first century is quite different from what is righteous in the twenty-first century. Paul, the rabbi, as expected, reflects the morality of the time and culture in which he lived and his Jewish background. The Jews currently believed that gentiles were immoral—Paul's catalogs of sins reflect current practices among some Gentiles—but the Gentiles were immoral because they did not believe in Yahweh and the covenant he struck with Abraham. Yes, their behavior was offensive, but if they had believed, then they would not have engaged in offensive behavior. That is, if they had believed in the covenant, they would not have been immoral because belief drives behavior, he, and most other people of his time and religious orientation thought. Then, believing communities were conceived as assemblies of saints, persons set apart by God for himself. Paul requires faith in a very straightforward manner for salvation, whereas he urges good deeds as in keeping with the status of being saved through faith. In other words, just as belief in the covenant would have made the gentiles moral, so, in the New Covenant, true faith logically (automatically?) leads to a life of good works. Therefore, faith alone assures salvation. *A great deal of time will pass before sin takes on a moral dimension, the way Christians today commonly view sin.* Nowadays, believing communities are more commonly thought of as congregations of sinners than as assemblies of saints.

The epistle to the Romans is commonly considered Paul's greatest, reflecting most clearly the state of his mind and theology towards the end of his life. So, we will continue to explore his gospel through Romans.

"But the words 'it was counted to him' were not written for his [Abraham's] sake alone, but for ours also. It will be counted to us who believe in him who raised from the dead Jesus our Lord, who was delivered up for our trespasses and raised for our justification. Therefore, since we have been justified by faith, we have peace with God through our Lord Jesus Christ."[10]

This is the good news (gospel) announced in this passage: God appointed Jesus as a scapegoat for our sins ("…Jesus our Lord, who was delivered up for our trespasses…"); God raised Jesus from the dead ("…and raised for our justification…"); if we believe that God raised Jesus from the dead, then we, too, shall be raised from the dead ("Therefore, since we have been justified by faith, we have peace with God through our Lord Jesus Christ.") Very straightforward, and, with patience, not too difficult to understand. All that is needed is faith once God set the plan of salvation.

"Paul, a servant of Christ Jesus, called to be an apostle, set apart for the gospel of God, which he promised beforehand through his prophets in the holy scriptures, concerning his Son, who was descended from David according to the flesh and was declared to be the Son of God in power according to the Spirit of holiness by his resurrection from the dead, Jesus Christ our Lord, through whom we have received grace and apostleship to bring about the obedience of faith for the sake of his name among all the nations, including you who are called to belong to Jesus Christ.

"To all those in Rome who are loved by God and called to be saints:

"Grace to you and peace from God our Father and the Lord Jesus Christ."[11]

Although this greeting at the beginning of the epistle has much in common with other greetings of Paul's epistles, it contains a number of ideas which we should bring to the front of our consciousness, lest we remain complacent in our culture. Paul claims that he was called to be an apostle. An apostle is a messenger, one who is sent on a mission. The term is sometimes used of the twelve whom Jesus gathered around him during his active ministry. Jesus in his lifetime did not appoint Paul an apostle, nor does Paul claim that he did. Paul does not refer to the earthly life of Jesus in any of his writings except for a brief reference to the last supper and references to the resurrection. Paul's office of apostle came from God.

---

10   Romans 4: 23-25; 5: 1.
11   Romans 1: 1-7.

Paul was "set apart" for the gospel of God. We know the story of Paul's conversion on his way to Damascus, as a result of which he became an apostle through a private revelation. (A private revelation is a revelation to a person who is not one of the twelve disciples of Jesus or the Apostle Paul. For what became the catholic church, only the teachings of the twelve and the preaching of Paul constituted the "deposit of faith," along with the New Testament texts which the church eventually approved. The deposit of faith embraces the fundamental, immutable core of teaching originating from God through Jesus. This teaching, according to their faith, was transmitted through the apostles to the bishops, who are now the monarchical leaders of the churches.) The proto-catholic congregations are identified as the very earliest congregations or churches which came to embody the several orthodox faiths. Their successors are collectively referred to as the catholic church. The catholic church later refused to accept private revelations as binding on the catholic church. In fact, even in the time of Paul private revelations contemporaneous with Paul's were rejected by many proto-catholic churches or congregations.

When Paul uses the term "holy scriptures," he is talking about the Hebrew Bible. Paul never quotes a gospel. In fact, all of the gospels were published after Paul died. To him, there are no "holy scriptures" besides the Hebrew Bible, not even his own epistles. As we shall see, he did not expect his writings to outlive him.

Paul states that Jesus was descended from David according to the flesh because he understood the prophets to say that the Messiah (Anointed One) would be descended from David. Therefore, in Paul's faith and gospel, Jesus was descended from David. Matthew and Luke give genealogies in their gospels which attempt to establish that Jesus was of the house of David, but for Paul, it seems to have been a matter of deductive logic from his faith.

Jesus was declared to be the Son of God *in power* by his resurrection from the dead. Recall that God raised Jesus from the dead. Therefore, God himself has adopted Jesus as his son. What we have here is strongly Adoptionist language. (Adoptionist: a theology which asserts that Jesus does not share the same substance as God [the Father].) Who, besides God, can declare that Jesus is the Son of God? God raised Jesus from the dead, and God adopted Jesus as his son. Keep this point in mind, as it will occur in theological disputes coming later. You will be exposed to the notion that theology shaped the scriptures of the New Testament, rather than the other way around.

Paul received "grace and apostleship" to bring obedience of faith to the Romans who are called to belong to Jesus. "Obedience of faith" may well refer to the good deeds which Paul believes are or should be characteristic of a believer. Paul understands "grace" as completely unmerited favor by God. If you re-read all the quotations from Paul which have preceded, or those which follow, you will find nothing to suggest that he or any other person could claim salvation through his own wits or works. His apostleship came from God, as his gospel (good news) came from God, not from Jerusalem, nor from James, the brother of Jesus and the apparent head of the Jerusalem congregation, nor from Peter. More on this later.

Paul wishes grace (favor) to the saints (the holy ones, that is, those persons set apart for Jesus) in Rome from God and Lord Jesus. In pre-Christian usage, something sacred was something set apart either for its estimable value or its horrid nature. Christians are set apart by God for salvation. Paul was set apart for the gospel of God.

It is important, if you wish to understand scripture, that your translations of scripture be "word for word," and that you understand the words as they were understood when the scripture was formed. This is not easy, but it is very rewarding.

"But now the righteousness of God has been manifested apart from the law, although the Law and the Prophets bear witness to it—the righteousness of God through faith in Jesus Christ for all who believe. For there is no distinction: for all have sinned and fallen short of the glory of God, and are justified by his grace as a gift, through the redemption that is in Christ Jesus, whom God put forward as a propitiation by his blood, to be received by faith."[12]

This passage follows an involved discussion of the Law as a manifestation of the righteousness of God. Here, Paul introduces a second manifestation of the righteousness of God. This new manifestation is God's offer of salvation for all who believe in God's

12 Romans 3:21-25.

righteousness through faith in Jesus Christ. This is a favor (grace), a completely unmerited gift from God. God has accepted the suffering and death of Jesus as atonement for our sins and offers that atonement—which is the practical meaning of "justification"—to all who believe through faith in Jesus' resurrection from the dead.

Jesus' resurrection from the dead was not seen as a one-time event: Paul saw it as the beginning of the parousia (the second coming of Christ). Jesus was exalted by God, assumed into heaven as a sign of God's acceptance of Jesus' sacrifice, and would soon return to earth to take with him to heaven all living believers and those who have died with faith in Christ.

Key Points

- Paul's "gospel" was not a written document. It was the "good news" (gospel) he preached to the Gentiles. To describe Paul's good news, modern scholars use the term "kerygma" rather than "gospel," because gospel has come to mean a written document about the ministry of Jesus. Kerygma is the preaching of a messenger or herald, with the emphasis on the message, not the preacher.
- Paul's good news was short and sweet:
    o God appointed Jesus as scapegoat for the sins of all who would believe in him.
    o God accepted Jesus' suffering as atonement for the sins of these believers.
    o God raised Jesus from the dead as a sign of his acceptance of Jesus.
    o God exalted (took up to heaven to sit at his right hand) Jesus, adopting Jesus as his son.
    o God grants salvation to all who "confess with your mouth that Jesus is Lord and believe in your heart that God raised him from the dead."
- Faith in the God who raised Jesus from the dead assures salvation, not works (good deeds). Salvation is a

completely unmerited favor from God, through faith in Jesus Christ.

- At the time of Paul, we know of no Christian church buildings. Paul sometimes preached in Jewish synagogues. There were congregations or groups of people who had similar feelings regarding the life and mission of Jesus. They met in the synagogues or in private residences, or both. The Greek word for "assembly, congregation" eventually became the word for "church."

- The congregations or churches differed in both beliefs and practices. More on this later.

- When Paul uses the term "holy scriptures," he is talking about the Hebrew Bible. To him, there were no "holy scriptures" besides the Hebrew Bible, not even his own epistles. He did not expect his writings to outlive him.

- Paul never quotes a gospel. In fact, all of the gospels were published after Paul died.

- Paul, the rabbi, believes that he, like the saints in Rome, is "set apart," or holy, or consecrated. This separateness reflects his Jewish culture. The Jews believed they were set apart, holy or consecrated, through God's pact with Abraham. The children of Abraham were God's "chosen people." More than most in the ancient world, Jews kept apart from society (to the extent practical), acted within their community, and maintained the singularity of their religious practices. That is, they excluded non-Jews from their society (to the extent practical). This exclusiveness was adopted by the proto-catholic congregations, that is, those churches which, over several centuries, adopted a monarchical system of governance, communicated with one another to promote similar views, forged a similar concept of "orthodox" beliefs, developed a common canon (rule) of scripture, and became the catholic (universal) church, which includes several theologically disparate orthodoxies.

The Time is Short

"Let every person be subject to the governing authorities. For there is no authority except from God, and those that exist have been instituted by God. Therefore whoever resists the authorities resists what God has appointed, and those who resist will incur judgment. For rulers are not a terror to good conduct, but to bad. Would you have no fear of the one who is in authority? Then do what is good, and you will receive his approval, for he is God's servant for your good. But if you do wrong, be afraid, for he does not bear the sword in vain. For he is the servant of God, an avenger who carries out God's wrath on the wrongdoer. Therefore one must be in subjection, not only to avoid God's wrath but also for the sake of conscience. For because of this you also pay taxes, for the authorities are the ministers of God, attending to this very thing. Pay to all what is owed to them: taxes to whom taxes are owed, revenue to whom revenue is owed, respect to whom respect is owed, honor to whom honor is owed.

"Owe no one anything, except to love each other, for the one who loves another has fulfilled the law. For the commandments, 'You shall not commit adultery, You shall not murder, You shall not steal, You shall not covet,' and any other commandment, are summed up in this word: 'You shall love your neighbor as yourself.' Love does no wrong to a neighbor; therefore love is the fulfilling of the law.

"*Besides this you know the time, that the hour has come for you to wake from sleep. For salvation is nearer to us now than when we first believed. The night is far gone; the day is at hand. So then let us cast off the works of darkness and put on the armor of light. Let us walk properly as in the daytime, not in orgies and drunkenness, not in sexual immorality and sensuality, not in quarreling and jealousy. But put on the Lord Jesus Christ, and make no provision for the flesh, to gratify its desires.*"[13]

Look again at the italicized (italics supplied) portion of Paul's preaching. In the latter fifties (when this epistle to the Romans was probably written), he is saying that the second coming of Christ is nearer than when he and his disciples first believed. This is the justification for the supine morality which he is preaching. Pay your taxes, defer to

---

13 Rom 13: 1-14. Italics supplied.

authority, make no provision to gratify the desires of the flesh, and so forth. To paraphrase this passage: don't worry about today's troubles; Jesus will very soon—"the night is far gone; the day is at hand"—come to make things right. (This expectation of imminent rescue from presently very difficult circumstances is called Apocalypticism, as in the alternative title for the book of Revelation, also called the Apocalypse.)

Paul says that the commandments are summed up in the injunction to love your neighbor as yourself. This continues Paul's logic that faith produces good works. Love of neighbor, which would fulfill the real requirements of the law, would be a natural (automatic?) consequence of faith in Jesus.

In any case, that good news makes sense only in the prospect of imminent apocalypse.

"I think that in view of the present distress it is good for a person to remain as he is. Are you bound to a wife? Do not seek to be free. Are you free from a wife? Do not seek a wife. But if you do marry, you have not sinned, and if a betrothed woman marries, she has not sinned. Yet those who marry will have worldly troubles, and I would spare you that. This is what I mean, brothers: *the appointed time has grown very short.* (Italics supplied.) From now on, let those who have wives live as though they had none, and those who mourn as though they were not mourning, and those who rejoice as though they were not rejoicing, and those who buy as though they had no goods, and those who deal with the world as though they had no dealings with it. For the present form of this world is passing away."[14]

In the early fifties Paul believed that the appointed time for Christ's second coming was very short. (Indeed, this whole letter to the Corinthians can be read as an exhortation to prepare for the parousia.) He saw the present form of this world as passing away. This sense of urgency is the only justification for the peculiar advice he just gave his listeners. Does it really make sense to make up an alternative to the world in which you really live? That is what he proposed. Change, the very hallmark of life through growth and adaptation, is discouraged. Make believe you don't want a wife if you are unmarried. If you are unhappy, make believe you are not unhappy. If you are happy, make believe you are not happy, and so forth. Why would one behave like that unless one expected radical change almost immediately?

---

14 I Corinthians 7:26-31.

"Rejoice in the Lord always; again I will say, rejoice. Let your reasonableness be known to everyone. *The Lord is at hand* (italics supplied); do not be anxious about anything, but in everything by prayer and supplication with thanksgiving let your requests be made known to God. And the peace of God, which surpasses all understanding, will guard your hearts and minds in Christ Jesus."[15]

In this more upbeat epistle, Paul urges rejoicing because the Lord (Paul's pet name for Jesus) is *at hand*. Don't worry about anything, he preaches. The time is short: we shall soon share with Jesus the glory of God.

We must distinguish between the meaning intended by Paul and the meaning taken by many people after the close of the first century, by more people after the close of the second century, and by almost everyone familiar with this passage after the close of the third century. Paul clearly states that the Lord is *at hand*. He and his followers shall see the righteousness of God displayed in the second coming of Christ in their lifetimes. Paul's preaching makes sense to his hearers. Future generations, however, come to adapt (the key to survival and the very thing Paul told them not to do) this time-line. Since Paul did not see the parousia, and since generations after Paul had not seen the second coming of Christ, the promise must not be time-specific. The notion of a particular judgment of a person at his death begins to develop. The promise must mean that at the end of a troubled life, God will make things right. Certainly, that is the belief widely held by oppressed people, slaves, serfs, many of those imprisoned by poverty and lack of opportunity, and so forth. Life cannot be meaningless: therefore God will rescue us. This theological development preserves the element of temporal proximity.

"But we do not want you to be uninformed, brothers, about those who are asleep, that you may not grieve as others do who have no hope. For since we believe that Jesus died and rose again, even so, through Jesus, God will bring with him those who have fallen asleep. For this we declare to you by a word from the Lord, that we who are alive, who are left until the coming of the Lord, will not precede those who have fallen asleep. For the Lord himself will descend from heaven with a cry of command, with the voice of an archangel, and with the sound of the

---

15 Philippians 4: 4-7.

trumpet of God. And the dead in Christ will rise first. Then we who are alive, who are left, will be caught up together with them in the clouds to meet the Lord in the air, and so we will always be with the Lord. Therefore encourage one another with these words."[16]

This description of what many call the "Rapture" does not point to the distant future. Paul and his contemporaries expected to participate in the Rapture. Two verses later he reminds his disciples that the day of the Lord will come like a thief in the night, that is, when you least expect it. Thus, all should be upright and vigilant because it could happen at any moment. Paul never imagined that his writings would survive him. His world was passing away.

It is important to keep in mind this Apocalypticism. We shall meet it again in the written gospels, and shall see that it is perhaps the single most important reason for the transformation of Christian congregations into Christian churches, and the transformation of the Greek word for "assembly, congregation" into the Greek word for "church."

Paul states that God will bring with Jesus those who have died in Christ. Are these Christians who have been unlucky enough to have expired before the parousia, or are they loved ones who have been baptized in the faith by the baptism for the dead referenced in I Corinthians 15: 29?[17] The question is important because the gospel of Paul has only one requirement for salvation: faith in the resurrection of Jesus Christ by God. If that faith must be asserted by a living person, then there is no hope for ancestors or heroes who have gone before. All those who predeceased Jesus have no hope of salvation, and only the fraction who have heard the gospel and believe can be saved.[18]

Key Points

- The resurrection of Jesus was not a one-time event. Paul believed it to be the beginning of a general resurrection of the dead and the end of the world as he knew it.

---

16 I Thessalonians 4: 13-18.

17 "Otherwise, what do people mean by being baptized on behalf of the dead?"

18 Thus, Cyprian may proclaim that there is no salvation outside of his narrow view of the church and intend this literally.

- Paul preached that the second coming of Christ was imminent: he and his disciples would be swept up to God with Jesus after Jesus joined with those who have "fallen asleep" in Christ.

- In view of the imminent parousia, his disciples should maintain their current status in life. The parousia is so close that to do anything would muddle the situation. Pay your taxes and your debts—all this is soon to go away.

- The injunction to "Owe no one anything, except to love each other, for the one who loves another has fulfilled the law" assumes faith in God, who raised Jesus from the dead. Righteousness is a consequence of faith.

- The present form of this world is passing away.

Origin of Paul's Gospel

If Paul tells us almost nothing about the earthly life of Jesus, he does little better telling us about himself.[19] He admits to having persecuted Christians, but outside of that there is almost no biographical information about Paul in his epistles. His reputation as an opponent of Christianity is mentioned in the *Acts of the Apostles* and his conversion to Christianity is narrated in *Acts* 9: 1-31. To find the origin of Paul' gospel, more properly, his kerygma, we have to go to his Epistle to the Galatians.

"Paul, an apostle—not from men or through man, but through Jesus Christ and God the Father, who raised him from the dead—and all the brothers who are with me,

"To the churches of Galatia:

"Grace to you and peace from God our Father and the Lord Jesus Christ, who gave himself for our sins to deliver us from the present evil age, according to the will of our God and Father, to whom be glory forever and ever. Amen."[20]

---

19   All discussion of Paul in this volume is restricted to the seven epistles which most scholars accept as genuinely written by Paul: Romans, I & II Corinthians, Galatians, Philippians, I Thessalonians, and Philemon.

20   Galatians 1: 1-5.

Paul, as always, claims to be an apostle, a messenger, one who was sent on a mission. But he does not owe his office to men. He is saying that his apostleship is not a result of a commission by James, the brother of Jesus and head of the Jerusalem congregation, or any other church leaders. (As a matter of fact, according to *Acts*, he starts preaching on his own initiative, without instruction or permission from church leaders in Jerusalem.)

But he goes boldly further: "Paul, an apostle—not from men *or through man*..." (italics supplied), by which he claims divine authority, explicitly stating that his apostleship came through Jesus Christ from God the Father. (The question of authority is central to the formation of the Christian churches and will be visited shortly below and more extensively again when discussing the emergence of the catholic church.) Authority doesn't get higher than Jesus Christ and God the Father who raised him from the dead.

When Paul proclaims that Jesus Christ gave himself to deliver us from the present evil age, he is proclaiming the apocalypse, preaching, "The end is neigh."

"For I would have you know, brothers, that the gospel that was preached by me is not man's gospel. For I did not receive it from any man, nor was I taught it, but I received it through a revelation of Jesus Christ."[21]

Again, Paul uses the generic term "man" to mean "humankind." He is again claiming divine authority for his kerygma, going on to state explicitly that he received his kerygma through a revelation of Jesus Christ.

In spite of Paul's claims of direct commission from Jesus Christ and God his Father, Paul's gospel was opposed by many members of the Palestinian churches.

Paul made a second visit to Jerusalem (because of a revelation), fourteen years after his first visit to James and Peter, to explain to them the gospel he was preaching to the gentiles. His kerygma differed from the kerygma of the Palestinian congregations in important ways. Paul did not impose the burdens of the Law (especially circumcision and dietary rules) on the gentiles. Palestinian congregations, being thoroughly Jewish, still by and large observed the Law and worshipped in the synagogues. Palestinian Christians saw themselves and were seen by their fellow Jews as another sect of Judaism, not as a separate religion.

---

21 Galatians 1: 11 f.

Palestinian Christians harassed Paul and his followers because they did not adhere to Jewish law. Paul speaks for himself about his visit.

"But even Titus, who was with me, was not forced to be circumcised, though he was a Greek. Yet because of false brothers secretly brought in—who slipped in to spy out our freedom that we have in Christ Jesus, so that they might bring us into slavery—to them we did not yield in submission even for a moment, so that the truth of the gospel might be preserved for you. And from those who seemed to be influential (what they were makes no difference to me; God shows no partiality)—those, I say, who seemed influential added nothing to me. On the contrary, when they saw that I had been entrusted with the gospel to the uncircumcised, just as Peter had been entrusted with the gospel to the circumcised (for he who worked through Peter for his apostolic ministry to the circumcised worked also through me for mine to the Gentiles), and when James and Cephas and John, who seemed to be pillars, perceived the grace that was given to me, they gave the right hand of fellowship to Barnabas and me, that we should go to the Gentiles and they to the circumcised. Only, they asked us to remember the poor, the very thing I was eager to do."[22]

Paul does not disclose the "revelation" which impelled his trip, but, given his designation of false brothers who slipped in to spy on him and to take away his freedom, it is reasonable to suppose that Judaizers were criticizing his gospel and harassing his disciples. So Paul went to Jerusalem to clear the air.

He did not approach the pillars, James, Cephas and John as a supplicant. It made no difference to him that these men seemed to be influential. He apparently laid out two gospels, one to the circumcised and one to the uncircumcised, and secured agreement, at least from the pillars, to this configuration.

This meeting, however, did not result in lasting peace, as we know from his later testimony. In fact, Peter and Paul had a falling out over the dietary rules.

"But when Cephas came to Antioch, I opposed him to his face, because he stood condemned. For before certain men came from James, he was eating with the Gentiles; but when they came, he drew back and

---

22 Galatians 2: 3-10.

separated himself, fearing the circumcision party. And the rest of the Jews acted hypocritically along with him, so that even Barnabas was led astray by their hypocrisy. But when I saw that their conduct was not in step with the truth of the gospel, I said to Cephas before them all, 'If you, though a Jew, live like a Gentile and not like a Jew, how can you force the Gentiles to live like Jews?' "[23]

Clearly, Paul does not fear Peter, and he firmly believes in the divine origin of his apostleship. But the passage says more: it implies that Peter (as well as Barnabas, Paul's companion, and other Jews) feared James, who apparently represented the circumcision party.

If the gospel to the circumcised made the Palestinian Christians look like a Jewish sect, the gospel to the uncircumcised looked like a new religion. Eventually these two groups merged, when the Jews began to expel Christians from the synagogues, but the process of expulsion probably took a decade or two over many different locations, starting after the time of a Jewish revolt which resulted in the destruction of Jerusalem and the Temple in the year 70.

Key Points

- Paul's gospel or kerygma comes from Jesus Christ and God the Father who raised him from the dead, not through any human commission.
- Paul's gospel or kerygma came to him and to him only: it was a private revelation which no one else shared.
- Paul's gospel was opposed by many members of the Palestinian congregations.
- Paul went to Jerusalem to confer with the pillars of the church, James, Peter, and John.
- They agreed on two gospels, one to the circumcised and one to the uncircumcised.
- The agreement did not hold, as members of Palestinian Christianity harassed Paul and his disciples.
- Paul was so secure in his position that he confronted Peter before an assembly of Jewish and gentile Christians.

---

23 Galatians 2: 11-14.

Chapter Three: Peter was a Jew

Did Peter Write a Gospel?

There is a document called the *Gospel of Peter*. The fragment we have is principally a narrative of the passion of Jesus. Some scholars believe it is the basis of the passion narratives in one or more of the canonical gospels. The gospel was cited, but not quoted, in ancient times by Justin Martyr (about 150), Origin (before 250), and Eusebius (around 300), but discovered only in 1886 in the tomb of a monk in Egypt. The gospel was accepted and used by some congregations. The date of composition is thought to be somewhere between 70-160. No modern scholar believes that the author is Peter the Apostle.

There is also a document called *Acts of Peter*, which, among other things, describes a miracle match between Peter and Simon Magus. Peter won, but *Acts of Peter* goes on to tell of his martyrdom. Its composition is believed to be somewhere between 150-200, well after Peter's death.

Another document, *Acts of Peter and the Twelve*, dates from 150-225. It is highly allegorical and somewhat strange, certainly to the modern eye. Peter is not the author.

Earlier (100-150) is the *Apocalypse of Peter*. This document, discovered in 1880, contains descriptions of heaven and hell revealed to Peter. Some scholars notice some commonality with the Second Epistle of Peter. The document was apparently popular and circulated widely. It is mentioned in the Muratorian canon (about 175) and was accepted as scripture by Clement of Alexandria. Then the *Apocalypse of Peter* drops out of sight, not to be cited or quoted until it was discovered in 1880. The idea of special revelations to the Twelve Apostles, who then passed these down to their appointed successors, was a very dear notion to the proto-catholic churches, but, alas, Peter is not the author.

II Peter (date of composition between 100-160) is considered a forgery by almost all biblical scholars. Content, style, self-references and even doctrinal issues lead them to this conclusion. The great Origin (third century) provides the first citation, even as he expresses doubts about its authenticity.

I Peter had generally been ascribed to the Apostle by ancient authors. The epistle was even then widely circulated and quoted. However, most modern scholars dispute Peter's authorship. One of the major reasons is the high quality of its Greek, judged to be just below that of *Hebrews* and *Acts*. *I Peter* also suggests a period of general persecution, which did not obtain through the period before it was quoted. (Nero's persecution was limited to Rome. There was a general persecution under Domitian about a quarter-century later.) It is addressed to gentile churches in Asia, churches with which Peter had no known relationship. Finally, the epistle seems to depend on the writings of Paul, especially *Romans* and *Ephesians*. The latter epistle is thought by many scholars to be a forgery, written by someone other than Paul after Paul's death. If so, the author of *I Peter* could not have been Peter the Apostle.

None of these documents constitute the gospel of Peter. Scholars have had to reconstruct the good news of Peter from the accounts of the genuine epistles of Paul, to a less extent from the *Acts of the Apostles*, and from whatever bits of history are known from other sources. Remember that in Galatians 2: 7 Paul said that they, the pillars of the congregation in Jerusalem, saw that he had been entrusted with the gospel to the uncircumcised, just as Peter had been entrusted with the gospel to the circumcised.

The congregations in Palestine were centered in Jerusalem, where James, the brother of Jesus, was head of one congregation, and Galilee, where the risen Jesus had instructed his followers to go. These were the first Christians. Somehow, they overcame the fear and despair caused by the crucifixion and labored on to preserve their memory of Jesus until he was seen to be Jesus Christ, the Anointed One, the Messiah.

If one reads the gospels, it is difficult to imagine that the first Christians were unorganized and confused as to the details of what just happened and the theological inferences of these events. We see the Resurrection and the accounts of the empty tomb as proximate causes of the faith of early Christians. But the gospels had not then been written; they represent later reflections on the disorganization and confusion which surely reigned. The Resurrection of Jesus and the accounts of the empty tomb can more readily be seen as *testaments* to the faith of early Christians, developed over time, rather than *causes* of their faith. As to the events which actually occurred, it is likely that we know more in the twenty-first century about the formation of Christian writings than the first Christians knew.

Papias, writing about 150, quotes an Elder.

"And the Elder said this also: Mark, having become the interpreter of Peter, wrote down accurately everything that he remembered, without however recording in order what was either said or done by Christ. For neither did he hear the Lord, nor did he follow him; but afterwards, as I said, (attended) Peter, who adapted his instructions to the needs (of his hearers) but had no design of giving a connected account of the Lord's oracles. So then Mark made no mistake, while he thus wrote down some things as he remembered them; for he made it his one care not to omit anything that he heard, or to set down any false statement therein…

"So then Matthew composed the oracles in the Hebrew language, and each one interpreted them as he could."[24]

Modern scholars are skeptical, in spite of the early date of this witness. For one thing, there is no evidence of a Hebrew source for Matthew's gospel. For another, there are more semiticisms in Mark's gospel than in Matthew's. And, of course, the names of Matthew and Mark were attached to these gospels long after they were written. (The proto-catholic congregations insisted upon apostolic sources for their valued writings.) Finally, Papias is the only witness to the gospels of Matthew and Mark before Justin Martyr, about 150.

One other conjectural point. "Oracles" are generally considered to be the mouthpieces of the deity or a deity. When Papias attributes oracles to Matthew, could it be a sayings list in Hebrew or, more probably, Aramaic? Some scholars think that Matthew's gospel is composed around five great discourses.

---

24   *The Apostolic Fathers*, p 529.

The events of the resurrection were in the minds of the women who stood by the cross. The men likely had fled. How the women's remembrances became scripture is a matter of conjecture, especially in light of the cultural bias against the testimony of women. In any case, the traditions written into the gospels we have today were likely not available to the first Christian men. The joy and certainty our culture emphasizes in reading these accounts de-emphasizes the doubts and uncertainty expressed in other gospel passages. The triumphal gospel, even including the doubting Thomas and other passages, very likely misrepresents the actual fear and cowering following the crucifixion. The stories of the empty tomb are probably apologetic appendages. Paul, the first documented Christian writer, firmly believes in the resurrection of Jesus, but he tells no tales of an empty tomb. Why should we expect more of the first Christians? Do we doubt the strength of their faith? These stories are not sources of their faith: these stories are witnesses to their faith.

These first Christians took their message (that Jesus was the Messiah) to other Jews in Jerusalem, Galilee, and to the Jewish *diaspora*, preaching in the synagogues, while themselves observing the Law. In Mt 5: 17-19, we read Jesus saying: "Do not think that I have come to abolish the Law or the Prophets; I have not come to abolish them but to fulfill them. For truly, I say to you, until heaven and earth pass away, not one iota, not a dot, will pass from the Law until all is accomplished. Therefore whoever relaxes one of the least of these commandments and teaches others to do the same will be called the least in the kingdom of heaven, but whoever does them and teaches them will be called great in the kingdom of heaven."[25]

It is unclear whether this pericope (a short passage or paragraph, especially referring to scripture) was written before Paul preached his gospel, or afterwards. However, since Paul preached his gospel some three decades before the gospel of Matthew was written, it is likely that this pericope was composed after Paul's kerygma, and was composed specifically to rebut it. The passage suggests that Paul was "the least in

---

25 One should remember that this admonition was directed at the written law as set down in the Torah or Pentateuch. At this time there was not universal or even nearly universal acceptance of "oral law," which *later* was described as given by Yahweh on Mt. Sinai, and which, *even later*, came to be written in the Babylonian and Palestinian (often called "Jerusalem") Talmuds.

the kingdom of heaven" because he advocated freedom from the Law. Worse yet, to other first Christians, Paul was the arch-heresiarch in claiming that works, that is, obedience to the Law, were not necessary to justify a Christian and could not justify a Christian. They understood Paul's position.

It appears that some of the first Christians believed that salvation could not be attained unless one fully observed the Law, including circumcision, the dietary laws and other obligations. This group is called "Judaizers." We have seen how the "circumcision party," strongly suggesting identification with James, the brother of Jesus, harassed the followers of Paul and Paul himself. We have seen how Peter waffled in the middle. Thus, there is a group among the first Palestinian Christians which believed in the legitimacy of the gospel of Paul, but which maintained that (Jewish) observant Christians are better Christians than non-observant Christians. And there is another group which believed that observance of the Law is necessary for salvation and that Paul was flat-out wrong. Diversity! at the very beginning of Christianity in the land of Jesus among his most devoted followers. This is a very important point which will be summoned again when we discuss the classical theory of heresy.

But there were not just two or three parties among the first Christians in Palestine. Different people held different beliefs about a host of issues. There was a continuum of beliefs among Palestinian Christians (just as there was among the gentile Christians). In the second century, we know of three gospels used by the Palestinian Christians, *Gospel of the Hebrews, Gospel of the Nazoreans,* and *Gospel of the Ebionites.* The congregations which used these gospels usually used the one of their liking exclusively or almost exclusively. They differed from one another in fundamental ways: was Jesus divine? to what extent must the Law be observed by Christians? is the virgin birth real?

It appears that the more extreme of the Judaizers held that Jesus was not pre-existent God who took on flesh, but he was merely the child of Joseph and Mary. They believed that God selected Jesus to suffer for the sins of all true believers because he perfectly observed the Law. This group of first Christians became known as Ebionites, and came to be branded heretics by some proto-catholic churches. This is a pattern to be repeated in many times and in many places: the first Christians of a congregation and sometimes the largest number of Christians in town found themselves branded as heretics, and, later, persecuted by the State in the name of good order.[26]

In the couple of decades immediately following the crucifixion, the first Christians in Palestine had developed no church offices as we know them. This does not mean that the congregations did not have leaders. The synagogues had leaders, and such would serve as the model for the Palestinian congregations to follow.

There is no early evidence of a priesthood. There is no early evidence of a monarchical bishop who alone held the sacerdotal powers to perform worship rites, to teach, to confirm, and so forth. They had no church buildings. They participated in synagogue worship, where they eventually came to teach that Jesus was the Messiah.

They may have gathered together on the Lord's day, Sunday—back then, every Sunday was Easter Sunday—and perhaps on another day or two during the week, but these developments likely took time to come into being and to become established. At these meetings, very likely in private homes, they would likely have read scripture, that is, the Hebrew Bible, to show how Jesus fulfilled the role of the prophesied Messiah. They may have sung psalms and hymns. They may have read letters from other Christian communities. There may have been revelation—prophesy—and speaking in tongues and interpretation of this speech, as there were in the gentile Christian churches established by Paul. They probably offered thanks (eucharist). They may have ended their meetings with a meal and a common acclamation: Maranatha! Come Lord Jesus! They expected Jesus at any moment.

Key Points

- None of the documents bearing the name of Peter, including the *Gospel of Peter*, the *Apocalypse of Peter*, or even the two epistles of Peter found in our New Testament were written by Peter the Apostle.

---

26   Bauer, Walter. *Orthodoxy and Heresy in Earliest Christianity*. (Fortress Press; Philadelphia, 1971.)

- The good news of Peter to the circumcised: Jesus is the Messiah promised by the (Jewish) prophets. The undeveloped nature of this kerygma testifies to its ancient age.
- The primitive congregations in Palestine embraced a continuum of beliefs and practices, just as did the gentile congregations of Paul. There no doubt was a pool of beliefs and practices held in common, deriving from similar experiences and kerygma, and many idiomatic beliefs and practices. There were, no doubt, differences within congregations.
- Congregations often preferred one gospel over the several others which eventually circulated.
- The processes by which the various documents of the New Testament were formed are not always clear. In any case, however, there were no documents we know of in the earliest times after the death of Jesus. The first published documents are the epistles of Paul, the earliest dating from about the year 52.
- Some in the Palestinian congregations felt that Paul and his followers were heretics.
- There is no evidence of a monarchical bishop or priesthood in very earliest Christianity.
- The congregations expected the imminent second coming of Christ. Maranatha!

Early Statements of Belief

Here are some of the earliest creedal statements in the New Testament.

"But we do not want you to be uninformed, brothers, about those who are asleep, that you may not grieve as others do who have no hope. For since we believe that Jesus died and rose again, even so, through Jesus, God will bring with him those who have fallen asleep. For this we declare to you by a word from the Lord, that we who are alive, who are left until the coming of the Lord, will not precede those who have fallen asleep. For the Lord himself will descend from heaven with a cry of command, with the voice of an archangel, and with the sound of the trumpet of God. And the dead in Christ will rise first. Then we who are alive, who are left, will be caught up together with them in the clouds to meet the Lord in the air, and so we will always be with the Lord. Therefore encourage one another with these words."[27]

"...yet for us there is one God, the Father, from whom are all things and for whom we exist, and one Lord, Jesus Christ, through whom are all things and through whom we exist."[28]

"For I delivered to you as of the first importance what I also received: that Christ died for our sins in accordance with the Scriptures, that he was buried, that he was raised on the third day in accordance with the Scriptures, and that he appeared to Cephas, then to the twelve..."[29]

"...concerning his son, who was descended from David according to the flesh and was declared to be the Son of God in power according to the Spirit of holiness by his resurrection from the dead, Jesus Christ our Lord...."[30]

"...for all have sinned and fall short of the glory of God, and are justified by his grace as a gift, through the redemption that is in Christ Jesus, whom God put forward as propitiation by his blood, to be received by faith..."[31]

"...It will be counted to us who believe in him who raised from the dead Jesus our Lord, who was delivered up for our trespasses and raised for our justification."[32]

"...because if you confess with your mouth that Jesus is Lord and believe in your heart that God raised him from the dead, you will be saved. For with the heart one believes and is justified, and with the mouth one confesses and is saved."[33]

---

27 I Thessalonians 4: 13-18.
28 I Corinthians 8: 6
29 I Corinthians 15: 3-5.
30 Romans 1: 3-4.
31 Romans 3: 23-25.
32 Romans 4: 24-25.
33 Romans 10: 9-10.

"For to this end Christ died and lived again, that he might be Lord both of the dead and of the living."[34]

"Great indeed, we confess, is the mystery of godliness:

"He was manifested in the flesh,

vindicated by the Spirit,

seen by angels,

proclaimed among the nations,

believed on in the world,

taken up in glory."[35]

"Remember Jesus Christ, risen from the dead, the offspring of David, as preached in my gospel..."[36]

"For Christ also suffered once for sins, the righteous for the unrighteous, that he might bring us to God, being put to death in the flesh but made alive in the spirit..."[37]

Key Point

- All of these early creeds are unambiguously Christological; none is unambiguously Trinitarian.

---

34 Romans 14: 9.

35 I Timothy 3: 16.

36 II Timothy 2: 8.

37 I Peter 3: 18.

Chapter Four: The Variety of Religious Experiences in Rome and Its Empire

Polytheism

The overwhelming majority of religious people in second century Rome embraced a wide variety of gods, some personal and familial, some celebrated by the state, most held in common with neighbors and the state. Whence came the gods?

The gods arrived with the evolution of humankind from pure animal to rationalizing animal. The pure animal lives in a chaotic world where things happen to it without advance notice and without any means, other than instinct, of avoiding calamity. On the other hand, the rationalizing animal begins to see associations between his behavior and events in his life.

The source of these associations is the rationalizing animal himself. The associations certainly exist in his mind, but they cannot be demonstrated to exist in the world outside of his mind. He projects onto animals, places, or things, his own apparent volitions and sentiments, giving them life and meaning in his existence. For example, thunderstorms can be frightening. Primitive man, fearing for his life, may attribute his safely passing through a frightening experience to the place at which he survived, making it a holy place or shrine. He may invest the place with a genius [38] at the spot where he was saved from

---

38 A divinity, perhaps inhabiting a thing or place. In pre-Christian times, genius connotes a divinity protecting an individual in the same manner as the Christian guardian angel, a personal tutelary spirit.

disaster. He knows that he did not save himself because he could not save himself from that superior power. He believes that he was saved by the genius.

Primitive man's reactions to darkness, fear, sudden noises, brilliant flashes, eclipses, and near death experiences are the wombs of the gods. A fearful prayer, a weapon, or an animal may take on a totemic[39] value.

These simplistic examples illustrate animism, probably the most widely practiced religion in the world, even today. Virtually all people act this way at one or more times in their childhoods, and many do so even in adulthood, in spite of professing another religion. Fear of ghosts, avoidance of the number thirteen, and countless other behaviors which we all have practiced sometime in our lives are examples of animism. In today's world, civilized populations are more likely to attribute their salvation to one of their gods or to their one God, but that merely reduces the number of overtly animistic reactions to life's events. It is not clear that attributing a stroke of good fortune to one's deity is materially different from animism when the claim is frequently repeated and one's god is lurking behind every stroke of good fortune. Less civilized populations are more naturally animistic as are children as opposed to adults.

Man grew up with a multitude of gods because there were a multitude of dangers, a multitude of opportunities, and a multitude of questions. If we, today, cannot conceive of more than one God, they, then, could not conceive of only one god.

Romans adopted, probably from the Etruscans, household gods, who had the limited duty of protecting hearth and home. They had no jurisdiction outside that household, but they were venerated by the family, usually at meals and at extended family gatherings, for fear that not to worship would result in loss or harm. *This is a central idea which characterized their society as well as their homes.* Their religion did not order them to worship. Their religion did not require any particular behaviors (morals). They worshiped because they had no control over their lives, and they believed that if they did not worship, the gods would be angry and not protect them from harm. They saw the gods as tutelary, that is,

---

39 Worship of or respect for an animal, less often a plant, less often a thing, which marks a group value.

supernatural powers watching over them and protecting them. In their worldview, that disposition made perfectly good sense.

The next step lay in anthropomorphism, treating the more important deities as having human form and character. This happened throughout the world inasmuch as rationalizing animals inhabited the world. Western culture particularly reveres Greek mythology. Here, the Greeks out shown the Romans, and, once the Romans conquered Greek colonies and the Greeks themselves, they adopted many of the Greek legends, Latinizing the names of the gods.

In second century Rome, we find an Empire which is naturally and sensibly polytheistic. People, including emperors, slaves, senators and plebes were largely fatalistic: what will be will be. Excluding Jews and Christians, to imagine a single provident God almost surely occurred to someone somewhere sometime in the second century, but he probably didn't talk about his idea for fear of ridicule, and if he did talk about it, he was probably ridiculed. And, the next loss or stroke of ill fortune he incurred was likely to be attributed to his atheism. Yes, atheism: he did not worship the gods.

Neither the Romans nor the Greeks were stupid peoples. The fact that they believed in many gods, the most important of whom often looked and acted like men and women, simply reflects their state of religious thinking, the point in time of their growth and achievement on the learning curve of theology.

Polytheism was amoral. There were no dietary laws or rules of behavior. Venereal pleasure was a free good, like air and water, to be enjoyed up to the limits imposed by elders, society, or the state. Religion imposed no limits.

Polytheism used no creeds. It did not require a particular set of beliefs. As a private matter, one could skeptically refuse to worship the gods, risking life and fortune, but this would have been a private decision. That is not the case with public celebrations and with the cult of emperors which developed in the first century.

Of course the gods must be worshipped in public. It was a citizen's duty to worship the gods. Otherwise the army might be defeated, a weather disaster might overwhelm the nation, a plague might break out, drought might play havoc with crops, in short, society could suffer great harm. To refuse to worship the gods amounted to atheism and treason, a desire to injure society and fellow citizens. (This type of civic religion is highly valued by governments even today. Witnesses: the Pledge of Allegiance, the National Anthem, the flag button. There is not a great deal of patience for those who refuse to pledge or sing, and nearly every aspirant to public office sports a flag button. Civil religion rules!)

It should be easy to understand why Christians were labeled atheists and traitors when they refused to worship the gods. Tacitus tells us that Christians were accused of the crime of hatred of humankind. The polytheists were perfectly willing to allow the Christians to practice permitted religions undisturbed, as long as they supported the state. Many forms of Christianity, however, required martyrdom of their adherents in preference to worshipping the emperor or to eating meat which had been sacrificed to idols. How could these people be seen as anything other than treasonous for inviting the destruction of society? Do not governments uniformly punish traitors?

It was not always so. The Romans had a poor understanding of this new religion in its early years. It was perceived, correctly for the first decades in Palestine, as another sect of Judaism. Usually, the Jews were not required by the Romans to worship Roman gods because their religion was seen as ancient. This "grandfather" exemption applied to this new sect of Judaism in some places for an unknown period of time. Paul's congregations, however, were rather quickly recognized as a new religion and rarely received protection because of their Jewish origin.

Polytheism survives today formally in the Hindu religion, one of the three great—in terms of the number of adherents—religions of the world. Practical polytheism survives informally throughout the world in nominally Christian societies, nominally Muslim societies, and among unbelievers wherever superstition, fate, or animism are proximate causes for particular behaviors.

Key Points

- Humans responded to the fears and uncertainties around them by projecting their individual emotions, desires, and sentiments upon things, places and animals. These genii assumed supernatural dimensions in the minds of those who created them out of a firm knowledge that they themselves could not control their own lives.

- Polytheism is a natural development on the path of civilization.
- The religious practices of Rome (and other civilizations) required citizens to preserve the commonwealth by participating in the public worship of the gods, even as we today require outward manifestations of the civic religion we call patriotism.
- Christians adopted the exclusiveness of their parent religion, Judaism. When, however, the Romans recognized Christianity as a religion separate from Judaism, it lost Judaism's protection as a religion approved for practice and became an illicit religion.
- Many Christian congregations, especially the proto-catholic, rejected compromise and insisted on martyrdom.

Mystery Religions

Mystery religions earned their name by requiring oaths of secrecy from members upon their initiation into the religion. In general, the mystery religions imported foreign gods, at least once officially by the state, but usually through more natural sources like curiosity or immigration. Although there is variety as to sources—Asia Minor, Egypt, Greece—there are similarities in their developing worldviews or theologies.

Mystery religions filled deep emotional needs. The prevailing view held that the wheel of fortune (chance) or fate (the Zodiac, stars or planets) deprived persons of any important control over life. These religions, along with Christianity, offered an escape. Adherents of the mystery religions were, in general, the few, the wealthy, and the well born.

The Eleusinian cult was one of the oldest and most widespread mystery religions. It developed from a myth about Demeter (Latin name, Ceres, whence, cereal), the goddess of agriculture, and her daughter, Kore (Latin name, Persephone). Briefly, Hades (Latin name, Pluto), the god of the underworld, kidnaps Kore and carries her off to the underworld to be his wife. There, Hades and Kore have a child, Plutus (wealth, from grain?). Demeter, distraught at her loss, forbids crops to grow while she searches for Kore. She searches far and wide, but in vain. Meanwhile, humankind suffers, as do the gods since the humans are not making their customary offerings. The gods prevail upon Hades to return Kore to Demeter, with the agreement that she will spend one-third of the year (winter) with him as his wife. Demeter allows the crops to grow and humankind and the gods are happy again.

The worldview follows the myth rather faithfully. Grain, the offspring of the ground, is reaped or raped to provide bread for humankind, offerings to the gods, and seed for the next crop. So Kore, standing in for all young women, is ravished to produce new offspring. The hope is this: when a person is buried, he is like a seed: he will grow again to participate in the cyclic renewal of life. (Provided, of course, he knows the right things and belongs to the right religion.)

Another very old (about 600 BCE) mystery religion is Orphism. It held that the body was a tomb encapsulating the soul. The soul was part of the divine. The only way the soul could escape was through asceticism: no meat, no wine, no intercourse. At the end of life, the soul was held either in a place of punishment or in the Elysian Fields, depending upon the quality of the life lived, before being incarnated again into another tomb (body). When the soul had lived a good life three times, it was reunited with the divine and released from the life cycle.

Other popular mystery religions included the cults of the Great Mother, Cybele (Asia Minor), Isis and Osiris (Egypt), Mithra (Persia) and Dionysius (Greece, Latin name Bacchus). While it is difficult to ascertain with certainty the elements of each religion's ritual, the following elements, except for Dionysian (Bacchanalian) festivals, would probably be found most of the time.

- A period of preparation for initiation. This would likely include fasting and abstinence from intercourse.
- An oath of secrecy.
- Confession of faults.

- Baptism.
- Initiation. This process almost surely would have involved mock death and rebirth.
- Services could include prayers (including prayers for the Emperor and the Empire), incense as sacrifice, and music (hymns).

Mystery religions are very old, but their popularity seems to have increased more rapidly during the first three centuries of the common era. Formerly, scholars thought that these religions may have helped to shape Christianity, but that view has changed. It is possible that the social and political conditions which abetted the growth of the mystery religions also abetted the growth of Christianity, but the latter is now viewed by most scholars as completely independent from the former.

Key Points

- Mystery religions imported foreign gods who, adherents believed could satisfy their unmet need for some control over their lives.
- Major themes included rebirth after death and release of the soul from the tomb of the body.
- Although mystery religions are very old, they seemed to have had a burst of popularity during the first centuries of the common era.
- Christianity appears to be quite independent of the mystery religions, but the political and social conditions which helped to popularize the mystery religions may have helped the spread of Christianity.

Gnosticism

Gnosticism is a philosophy originating more than five centuries before the common era. It developed over time, and Plato himself added to its vocabulary. By the time Christianity emerged, Gnosticism

53

was ready and able to interpret the Christian message in its own terms. In fact, it may be plausibly claimed that Gnostics were the first Christian systematic theologians, and Gnosticism forced the theological development of proto-catholic Christianity.

The name Gnosticism is a modern appellation from the Greek word *gnosis*, which means knowledge. For Gnostics, the knowledge was secret knowledge because it was very difficult to obtain, beyond the ability of most humans. Gnosticism has always been elitist, an important point to keep in mind.

The basic tablature posits a God, pure spirit, who emanates his divine nature into separate persons. These emanations, called aeons, contain something of the divine essence, the first emanation containing the purest expression of the divinity, the second, only slightly less pure, and so forth. Christ was the first emanation according to Christian Gnostics, and he would provide the secret knowledge to those relatively few who had searched inside themselves for their spark of divinity.

The aeons expressed attributes of the godhead. Eventually, however, the emanations became impure enough to admit error. An errant aeon created the physical universe, an abortion of the pure spirit, wholly alien to God, and wholly evil.

Gnosticism is a dualistic system of thought, pure spirit, God, over against the physical world, pure evil. Evil, the physical world, resulted from a break with the godhead.

Plato's contributed his use of the word "demiurge" to describe the subordinate god who arranged the physical world to conform to a rational and eternal idea. The demiurge takes the preexisting material of chaos and constructs a physical world which mirrors eternal forms or ideas. It seems that Plato was de-emphasizing the evil nature of the physical world while still maintaining the excellence of the godhead, pure spirit, the ideal, the idea. While Plato saw the demiurge as, perhaps, the symbol of rationality, some later Christian Gnostics identified the demiurge with Yahweh, the god of the Jews, the evil creator of the evil world.

Humans retained some small spark of divinity within themselves. With great effort, they could find that spark, and Christ would then reveal to them secret knowledge leading to salvation, that is, reunification with the godhead. At least one Gnostic group read the story of Adam and Eve as precisely two such persons seeking to be reunited with God, the Father, First God, when they ate the fruit from the tree of knowledge of good and evil. Yahweh, the least aeon, the evil god of material creation, banished them from the Garden and cursed them.

Nor is Gnostic revelation the same as philosophical enlightenment because it cannot be acquired by reason or by reading. It requires introspection, and, perhaps, some education to know how to examine oneself and the surrounding world with profit. Most people were deemed by Gnostics to be unequipped to undertake this journey.

Nor is Gnostic revelation the same as Christian revelation. Jesus and his revelation are historical events. Gnostic revelations, on the other hand are individual and personal, wholly interior to the person himself.

When Christianity emerged, Gnosticism had been around for centuries, ready with a vocabulary and concepts to interpret the events of the first century. On the other hand, the first Christians possessed the limited vocabulary of Judaism, an exclusivist sect often out of touch with much of the world in which it existed. Christianity had no system of philosophy with which to interpret events. The irruption of the Christian experience had little to do with Judaism, as events would show, and Christians had to develop a vocabulary to express their theology.

But, Christians believed that the world was soon going to end. If a man were unmarried, he was advised not to marry, and so forth. Christians considered theological speculation unimportant, perhaps even worldly and vain. This world was passing away. Jesus would come soon. The core of Christian belief, apocalypticism, abetted the development of Gnostic theological speculations and retarded the development of theology among the proto-catholics.

One may fairly say the Gnostics were the first Christian theologians: they brought an orderly system of thought to bear on the Jesus experience. The Christian apologists of the second, third, and fourth centuries were reacting, in the main, to Gnostic theology. The Christian attempts to define a canon of scripture were, again, a reaction to Gnostic assertions regarding which writings should be considered authoritative. The first canon of scripture was proposed by a Gnostic. The Christian canon as it exists today would not be defined for more than two hundred years afterwards. Even the development of the office of monarchical bishop should be seen as a defense (apology) to the assertion that individual human beings can be in touch with the godhead.

Key Points

- Gnosticism is an ancient philosophical system, dualistic in nature, posing spirit (good) against matter (evil).
- Gnostics held that God did not create the world. God is pure spirit, utterly good. The world is almost pure matter, utterly evil. To counter this assertion, proto-catholic churches included acknowledgement of God, the Father, as creator of heaven and earth in the creeds developed in the second through the fifth centuries.
- However, a relatively few individuals, through thoughtful introspection, can uncover the slight spark of divinity within them, and Christ, pure spirit, will then reveal to them the path to reunification with the divine.
- Gnostics are in touch with God. No intermediary is possible. Each knows God in a manner in which no other person, not even a monarchical bishop, can know God.
- Gnostics, to support their theological speculations, proposed the first canon of scriptures.

Judaism

There is no need to repeat the summary of Judaism in chapter one except to stress that a Jew could be one of at least nine different kinds of Jew, a Sadducee, a Pharisee, an Essene (religious viewpoints, including the party which has survived to become modern Judaism), and in the Christian era before expulsion from the synagogues, a Nazarene, an Ebionite, or a Cerinthian (all religiously different groups with shades of meaning within each group), a Zealot, a Herodian or a Samaritan (political groups rooted in religious outlooks).

Early Christian Congregations in the Empire

Palestinian Christians

Through the fourth century and, in some cases, beyond, each Christian community seemed to treasure one gospel more than the others. At least three different gospels were in use among Palestinian Christians in the second and third centuries, the *Gospel of the Hebrews*, the *Gospel of the Nazoreans*, and the *Gospel of the Ebionites*. This suggests plurality in beliefs and practices among Jewish-Christian congregations. In fact, the first Jewish-Christian congregations were seen as sects of Judaism rather than a new religion. The previous chapter discussed the beliefs of the Ebionites. Non-Ebionite congregations would have been less rigid with respect to observance of the Law, some, perhaps, excusing gentiles altogether from compliance.

The presence of these groups does not mean that proto-catholic and Gnostic congregations did not exist among Palestinian Christians. In fact, one of the first Gnostic Christians was a Samaritan, Simon Magus. It is possible that several proto-catholic congregations existed in Palestine. Thus, the native land of Jesus sprouted very diverse congregations of Christians under the noses of, and probably with the help of Jesus' closest companions.

Proto-catholic Christians

The catholic church came into being through the struggles of proto-catholic congregations to understand and to pass on what they believed had been given to them by Jesus and the Apostles. Many of these congregations struggled with other proto-catholic congregations because of differences in their understandings of what they received. But most of all, virtually all proto-catholic congregations were reacting to a host of Gnostic Christian congregations whose understanding of Jesus, Jesus' message, God, and the world itself differed in remarkable ways from theirs. They believed that what they had received came from Jesus himself or from those most closely associated with him. They saw Gnosticism, a pagan philosophy, insinuating Christianity and perverting its message. The exclusivism adopted from their Jewish forbearers boiled over into the charge of heresy. They alone knew the truth, even though it had not yet been clearly defined. They did not accept Gnostics as being Christian.

It was imperative for them to preserve the true message, tending toward the designation "orthodox." It was imperative for them to expose the false (heterodox) beliefs of the Gnostics. Proto-catholic congregations had to band together, had to communicate with one another, had to forbear differences among allies for at least a time.

Apocalypticism was the common expectation of early Christians. Some second generation Christians and most third generation Christians reflected upon their communities. These congregations came to believe that they had something worth passing on, something which must be preserved. They began to be concerned about eschatology, the study of the last four things, death, judgment, heaven and hell. They were experiencing an increasingly severe eschatological problem: what was taking so long for Jesus to return? They needed to write down what they remembered the Lord said and did. They needed to organize to a degree they had not organized before, otherwise their experiences, which they considered to be of supreme value, to the point of martyrdom, would be lost to future generations.

In the early second century, there is evidence of the formation of church offices. (Unless one believes that Acts was composed in the second century, the appointment of seven deacons described in *Acts* 6: 5 does not describe a church office, but rather, the first century version of meals on wheels.) The development of the office of bishop is difficult to discern, but it appears that some or many bishops assumed monarchical or near monarchical powers by the mid or late second century, Rome probably being the first, and probably a little earlier. It appears that bishops were independent one from another, and that they were usually chosen by consensus of the community, or, at least, community leaders. By the fourth century, major churches, such as Alexandria and Antioch, tended to lead the bishops surrounding them. The Council of Nicea (325) raised the status of the church at Rome to that of the church at Alexandria.

Gnostic Christians

Once the catholic church became the state religion of the Empire, its opponents were persecuted out of existence, where that was possible.[40] Their writings were burned or otherwise destroyed. Writings which hinted of Gnosticism, if not destroyed, were not copied, consigning them, usually, to oblivion. As a result, what we knew of Gnostic Christians came from apologists of the proto-catholic point of view. That is, what we knew about Gnostics was written by their bitter enemies. We know some were bitter by the intemperate language and personal attacks in their writings.

In 1945, a trove of ancient Gnostic writings was discovered in Egypt. This discovery has materially enhanced our understanding of the Gnostic Christians. We must, however, rely on their enemies with respect to most of the details which follow.

Simon Magus

Simon Magus, a native of Samaria, amazed people with his magic and miracles. According to a story contained in *Acts* 8: 9-24, Simon converted to Christianity. When he witnessed Peter and John laying hands on the newly baptized and conferring the Holy Spirit, he was amazed at their power and offered to purchase that power from them. Peter condemned him roundly, although he later reconciled after Simon repented.

Justin Martyr in the second century reports that Simon visited Rome. His magic was wildly popular, and, according to Justin, his followers deified him. Irenaeus calls Simon the first Gnostic Christian.

Some third century Christian documents picture Simon as a false Messiah. The *Acts of Peter* have him contending with Peter in a miracle match. Another legend has Simon falling to his death from the top of the Roman Forum as he was demonstrating his ability to fly.

Justin and Irenaeus recount the Simonian creation myth. God the

---

40   The state was not interested in religion *per se*, but it was interested in peace and stability, that is, one religion. This thinking obtains today. In democracies, civil religion (patriotism) becomes the glue which is to overcome religious differences.

Father, or First God, created Ennoia, the first thought, a female. Ennoia created the angels, who, in turn, created the physical universe. These angels imprisoned Ennoia in human bodies so that she could not return to the Father. Ennoia is reincarnated over and over, but cannot escape. Simon Magus descended from heaven to redeem Ennoia in her last incarnation, Helen, Simon's consort. The very sharp dichotomy between spirit and matter seems somewhat muted among his followers.

Cerinthus

Cerinthus, who flourished around the turn of the first century, was a Palestinian Gnostic Christian. He used the *Gospel of the Hebrews* and followed Jewish Law. Cerinthus denied that the supreme God had created the world, denied the divinity of Jesus, distinguished between Jesus and Christ, affirmed that Christ entered Jesus at his baptism, guided his ministry, and stayed with him until his crucifixion, exiting before Jesus died since God could not suffer death.

Basilides

Basilides taught philosophy in Alexandria about the years 117–138. It is believed that he wrote more than twenty-four books of commentary on the Christian gospels, but not one has survived. Basilides taught that faith comes from nature, not from will. He believed and taught transmigration of the soul (metempsychosis), and that evil experiences in this life may be payback for evil the soul performed in a previous life. In fact, he taught that the only penalty for evil deeds in life is to have the soul live another life in another body. The real penalty, apparently, was failure to reunite with God.

Thus, martyrdom could be a just punishment for a past sin. Basilides cited Romans 7: 9 as proof: "I was once alive apart from the law, but when the commandment came, sin came alive and I died."

Marcion

Marcion, who flourished in the first half of the second century, was the first known Christian to propose a canon of scriptures. His canon, like future canons, was driven by theology. It consisted of one gospel, which contained about two-thirds of the *Gospel according to Luke* and the ten epistles ascribed to Paul which were known to him, excluding the pastoral epistles, *I & II Timothy* and *Titus*.

Marcion excluded the Hebrew Bible from his canon. Yahweh, the god of the Hebrew Bible was an evil god because he created matter, the visible universe. One merely must look around to see evil everywhere. The Hebrew Bible deserved no reverence as scripture.

To prove his point, he illustrated a number of contradictions between the testaments, like contrasting the command in *Joshua* to slay every man, woman and child in Jericho with the sermon in *Matthew* 5: 39-44 or *Luke* 6: 27-30 to love your enemy, turn the other cheek, and pray for those who persecute you.

Marcion insisted upon a literal interpretation of the Hebrew Bible. He pointed out that God did not know where Adam was in the Garden of Eden. Yahweh appeared to be ignorant. When Yahweh relented in destroying Sodom and Gomorrah for a time, he was indecisive. When he ordered Joshua to kill every living thing in Jericho, he manifested his cruelty. In promising harsh punishments against anyone who broke his laws, this god proved vindictive.[41]

Marcion introduced a new God, hitherto unknown, a God of goodness and light, of pure spirit, *totally benevolent*, wholly free from wrath and passion. Jesus was not the Messiah of the Hebrew Bible, whom he saw as a political leader or revolutionary. Rather, Jesus was a fellow Gnostic, a redeemer sent by God to free humankind from the tyranny of the flesh. Souls would be saved, not bodies: there would be no resurrection of dead bodies.

Marcion's hatred of matter led him, like many Gnostic groups, to an extreme asceticism. He denied the right to marry and proposed rigid rules for fasting.

Marcion had a wide following. He sought to become bishop of

---

41   See Ehrman, Bart D., *Misquoting Jesus* and *Lost Christianities*.

Rome, but, instead, was cast out of that church. The fact that he could contend to become bishop of Rome indicates the fluidity of theology in mid-second century Rome, not to mention the ways by which bishops were chosen. In spite of his disavowal of marriage, his group perdured for several hundred years.

Valentinus or Valentinius

Valentinus may have been the best known and most successful Gnostic Christian theologian. He was educated in Alexandria, supposedly under Theudas, a disciple of St. Paul. Valentinus claimed that Theudas shared with him secret knowledge which Paul shared with his inner circle.[42] In addition, this poet and mystic claimed to have had a vision of the risen Christ.

He founded his own school there which gained many followers throughout Egypt and the Near East. Around 136, he travelled to Rome, where again he founded a school which became quite popular and exercised influence. Valentinus hoped to become Bishop of Rome, but when he was passed over, he left that church and, later, perhaps, Rome itself.

Valentinus and his followers believed that only through secret knowledge could one be saved. Only mature Christians could understand the *gnosis*, and long periods of preparation may be necessary.

Mature Gnostic Christians communed directly with God, and, therefore, were equal in the sight of God. These Gnostic Christians generally remained members of their proto-catholic churches, and some Valentinians held church offices. In their private meetings, however, they traded church offices such that a deacon today might be a bishop next, and a reader at the following meeting. Women, of course, participated in all offices since all Christians were equal.

Proto-catholics began to excommunicate Valentinians in a few places where vigorous apologists held power rather early, but this practice was not uniform, and Valentinians remained in proto-catholic churches

---

42 "I know a man in Christ who fourteen years ago was caught up to the third heaven—whether in the body or out of the body I do not know, God knows. And I know that this man was caught up into paradise—whether in the body or out of the body I do not know, God knows—and he heard things that cannot be told, which man may not utter." II Corinthians 12: 2-4.

until the fourth century. When they were expelled, Valentinians formed their own communities and carried on for several hundred years.

Montanus

Around the year 175, Montanus worked signs and wonders under, he claimed, the influence of the Holy Spirit. He taught that the period of Revelation had not closed, and, indeed, that he and his followers were in touch with the Holy Spirit. He preached that women were prophets as well as men, and at least one of the two principal female prophets who accompanied him had an apparition of Christ in the form of a woman. (This, in an age when women were considered chattel, mere possessions of a father or a husband.) Like most Gnostic sects we know, his followers practiced an extreme asceticism. In fact, Tertullian, the brilliant proto-catholic apologist and perhaps father of church Latin, dismayed by the morals of proto-catholicism, joined the Montanists and became their chief apologist in the early 3rd century.

Carpocrates

Carpocrates and his followers were vilified by the proto-orthodox, who believed their worship services were sexual orgies. Clement of Alexandria, (ca. 200) describes them as sharing everything, including wives. Irenaeus claimed that Carpocrates taught that the body must be re-incarnated until it experienced all the things a body can experience; only then could the divine spark be released. Perhaps worship orgies were the plan for salvation: quick release.

Key Points

- In the homeland of Jesus a variety of Christianities grew and flourished, at least for a time.
- The early Christian congregations in Palestine were generally considered sects of Judaism, until the Jews expelled the Christians or the Christians left the synagogues.

- Some sects continued into the third and fourth centuries.
- Virtually all Christians expected Jesus to return soon, either to take them to heaven or, according to a later tradition held by others, to establish a kingdom on Earth.
- With the second and third generations of Christians, proto-catholic churches began to plan as to how they would pass on their heritage, teachings, and practices.
- Gnostic Christians developed theologies sooner than proto-catholics, putting pressure on proto-catholics to think systematically about their theology.
- Although there were a variety of Gnostic churches, it would be a mistake to assume that the proto-catholic churches were significantly more uniform in beliefs and practices than the Gnostic churches. These differences will be discussed in chapter eight.

Chapter Five: The Development of the Gospels, Part I

Ancient and Modern Writers:
More than Style is at Issue

The gospel of Matthew was not written by Matthew the Apostle; the gospel of Mark was not written by Mark, the companion to Peter the Apostle; the gospel of Luke was not written by Luke, the physician and companion of Paul, and the gospel of John was not written by the Apostle whom Jesus loved. These attributions arose much later than the gospel creations themselves, when the proto-catholic churches needed to reinforce their contention of unbroken transmission of teaching from the Apostles themselves or from trustworthy persons closely associated with them. Furthermore, there is evidence in the texts themselves that more than one person was responsible for the final form of the texts we have. The best candidate for single authorship, based on the high quality of the written Greek, is the Gospel according to Luke and its follow-on work, *The Act of the Apostles*. Let's start with Luke.

"Inasmuch as many have undertaken to compile a narrative of the things that have been accomplished among us, just as those who from the beginning were eyewitnesses and ministers of the word have delivered them to us, it seemed good to me also, having followed these things closely for some time past, to write an orderly account for you, most excellent Theophilus, that you may have certainty concerning the things you have been taught."[43]

---

43   Luke, 1:1-4.

What was the author of this gospel looking at or thinking of when he wrote these words? It is quite certain that he was familiar with the *Gospel according to Mark*, and some scholars believe that he was familiar with Matthew's gospel, although today that is a distinctly minority position.

Did he have available other gospel accounts which were omitted from the canon of scripture we have? Did he have a list of "oracles" composed in Hebrew by Matthew the Apostle mentioned by Papias (ca. 150)? More likely than either of these, he likely had a collection of sayings modern scholars call Q, from the German word, *quelle*, which means source. More about that later.

We have seen that Paul's gospel was not a written gospel but the good news of salvation he preached to the gentiles. Similarly, Peter never wrote a gospel but preached good news. In the second chapter of *Acts*, Peter is depicted as giving a long sermon on the occasion of the descent of the Holy Spirit upon the Apostles. In the third chapter of *Acts*, Peter is again pictured as delivering a long sermon on the occasion of having cured a lame man in the Temple precincts. When you recall that ancient authors usually composed the speeches they put into the mouths of their subjects, you can appreciate why some scholars point to these sermons as bridges from kerygma, preaching the good news, to gospel, as written good news in the form of a narrative about Jesus. How can that be? Wasn't *Acts* written after the Gospel according to Luke? (*Acts* and Luke's Gospel could have been broken apart to permit insertion of John's Gospel.)

It is unlikely that Peter ever made either speech. Luke, to use that name as a placeholder for the anonymous author, as we shall use Matthew, Mark and John similarly, had available to him some document(s) or tradition(s) about Peter at about this time—although chronological congruence is not strictly required for ancient writers—and Luke composed and put into Peter's mouth these sermons. Ancient historians did this all the time. Calls to arms and victory speeches are the creations of the authors, not the speakers. If this is the case here, then one can see how the earlier document(s) or tradition(s) can be a bridge from kerygma to written gospel.

The constructed speeches represent oral (probably) or written traditions received by Luke and put forth in *Acts* as written narratives. This is very likely the process by which the gospels were formed. Individual oral traditions were written as narratives, speeches, miracle stories, pronouncement stories, and so forth, and preserved in idiosyncratic communities. As faith in the Jesus story overcame fear and doubts, these stories were shared in oral, and later, written form. It is probable that these stories were embellished and extended. Then came Mark. He strung the pearls together, as had others (the Q document, the *Gospel of Thomas*, some narratives of the passion of Jesus, and others). These are discussed in the following chapter.

It is very important to note that when Luke put these speeches into the mouth of Peter, Luke was not intending to deceive. He was observing the conventions of his time. His contemporaries did the same thing. The only problem occurs when we expect modern standards to apply to ancient writings.

Since we are in *Acts*, it would be fruitful to point out several other issues in these first chapters simply because we are here, and because these are the kinds of issues which arise in the development of the gospels.

In verse four of chapter one of the *Acts*, Jesus instructs the Apostles not to leave Jerusalem. This is consistent with Luke's Gospel (24: 49) where he instructs the Apostles to remain in Jerusalem until they have received "...power from on high." Luke (24: 6) harmonizes this instruction by having the young men at the empty tomb telling Mary, "Remember how he told you, while he was still in Galilee..." This, however, does not comport with Mark, 16: 7: "...but go, tell his disciples and Peter that he is going before you to Galilee." Matthew is more emphatic: Matthew 28: 7; 9 & 10; and 16 picture Jesus telling the disciples three times to go to Galilee.

These details are probably not a major issue for most Christians, but the details reflect the problem of scholars (1) in tracing sources for the different traditions, (2) evaluating the traditions, and (3) constructing a text which reflects the writer's original understanding of events, (4) reconstructing the text he wrote, and (5) understanding the meaning he intended to convey.

Acts 1: 3 has Jesus ascending to sit at the right hand of the Father on the fortieth day after his resurrection. No other account of the ascension, including that found in Luke's gospel, is so precise. Forty days after resurrection Sunday will always fall on a Thursday. Exactly ten days later comes the Holy Spirit, the power from on high mentioned by Luke. It falls on a Sunday, the celebration day adopted early by Christians, exactly fifty days after the resurrection, and becomes Pentecost Sunday. Pentecost is a Jewish celebration beginning fifty days after the second day of Passover (the beginning specified for a liturgical reason). Now we have a Christian celebration fifty days after the resurrection, both the resurrection and pentecost falling on the Christian celebration day.

It is difficult for modern scholars not to detect a construct behind this narrative, as if the narrative were developed to fit a story the author wanted to tell. This assumption may be wholly unjustified in terms of the author's knowledge and intentions, but this approach illustrates the scholar's quest for the original text the author wrote, the writer's original understanding of events, and the meaning he intended to convey.

Continuing with the pentecost narrative (*Acts* 2: 1-4), the Holy Spirit descends upon the Apostles in the form of divided tongues of fire resting on each one of them. "And they were all filled with the Holy Spirit and began to speak in other tongues as the Spirit gave them utterance."

Paul's epistles mention speaking in tongues and interpreting tongues several times. However, the catholic churches later forbade this practice for several reasons. First, speaking in tongues suggested that a member of the congregation was in direct communication with the Holy Spirit. The catholic churches, while not denying that such communication is possible, denied that such communication could be authenticated by the church. Therefore, such a communication could not be used in liturgical devotions or as a source of continuing revelation. Second, which is really first in the minds of the bishops, the bishops alone, they believed, were the source of the authentic teachings of Jesus the Christ, and, therefore, God. These two points illustrate the development of theology. What was licit at one time becomes illicit later as theological speculation develops a new understanding of what the writings which later became scriptures really meant. Third, good order in liturgical celebrations involves restraint and dignity, neither of which is served by enthusiasm.

Continuing in *Acts* (2: 5-12), the Apostles, filled with the Holy

Spirit, attracted a crowd of people from "every nation under heaven," and each of these people heard the message of the Apostles in his own language. Granted that the hyperbole of "every nation under heaven" is simply a figure of speech, the miracle of understanding each in his own language requires faith. To the best of our knowledge, nothing like this has happened in the rest of recorded history.

Scholars, by definition, should be persuaded by evidence. On balance, scholars might be more inclined to suggest that at least this portion of *Acts* has a theological purpose. It is doing what John, in his gospel (20: 30-31), said, "Now Jesus did many other signs in the presence of his disciples, which are not written in this book; but these are written so that you may believe that Jesus is the Christ, the Son of God, and that by believing you may have life in his name." The purpose of this pericope is to illustrate the mighty works of God so that the reader is led to faith. There may be another purpose, to provide an account of what actually happened, but, in the view of many, the evidence of theological purpose diminishes historical reliability.

For Luke, there may have been an important connection to the twelve Apostles and the twelve tribes of Israel, like the connections between the Jewish agricultural festival of pentecost and the Christian celebration of pentecost. He relates in *Acts* 1: 21-26 the choosing of the successor to Judas to fill out the twelve. Two men were proposed, Barsabbas and Matthias. They are described as "...men who have accompanied us all the time that the Lord Jesus went in and out among us, beginning from the baptism of John until the day when he was taken up from us—one of these men must become with us a witness to his resurrection."

Neither of these men is known to us before this passage. Thus, it is difficult for us to understand how they could have been constant companions of Jesus and witnesses to the resurrection. Note that the candidates were chosen by consensus, not appointment. Furthermore, the selection of the successful candidate was presumed to occur by an act of God speaking through a throw of the dice. Neither of these actions is evidence of a monarchical bishop.

It is not clear how the Apostles knew that prayer would guide the lot to give them the better man for the job. Perhaps they were driven by faith. While that assumption is perfectly plausible, modern scholars would see this selection process as flawed. There is no way to connect the will of God to a throw of the dice without a specific revelation. On the other hand, if there had been a revelation, there would have been no need to throw dice.

Key Points

- The gospels are anonymous. They are not forgeries (pseudepigrapha); Matthew did not claim to write the gospel attributed to him, and the same goes for Mark, Luke and John. None of the evangelists claims to be an eyewitness. There are no first person accounts, such as "I went with Jesus to…" We simply do not know who wrote them: the authors are anonymous.
- It is very difficult to know what resources were available to the authors of the gospels. We have to infer their sources from the gospels themselves and whatever other few clues may be available.
- To apply modern standards to ancient texts will very likely lead to misunderstandings, some of which may be very important.
- The first chapters of *Acts* provide lessons on the difficulty of understanding gospel texts:
  o The first step involves understanding the source of the tradition behind the text.
  o Then the tradition must be evaluated across several dimensions.
  o Then we must infer what the author understood about the events he describes.
  o Then one may try to construct a text which reflects the writer's original understanding of the events he reports.
  o Finally, sitting in his time and place, we must reconstruct the message he intended to transmit.
- In addition, other problems present themselves.

o Texts sometimes appear to contradict each other.

o Some pericopes seem to be constructions of the author, that is, narratives developed to illustrate a theological point.

o As time passes and new issues present themselves, the development of theological speculation leads to changes in the words of scripture— see below—and to the interpretation of scripture.

o When an author's theological purpose is evident, many readers proceed with caution in evaluating the pericope's historical reliability.

o The use of lot to pick a successor to Judas is curious to the modern mind. Furthermore, it is an illustration of the actual state of church governance sixty or more years (when this account was written) after the death of Jesus. There is no evidence of a monarchical bishop, candidates for office were chosen by consensus, and God was expected to speak through lot.

o We do not have the original texts (autographs) of the gospels. What we have are copies of copies, and, as we shall see, none too carefully copied.

The Gospel of John

If Luke's writings are the most likely candidates for single, pure authorship, John's gospel shows clear evidence of having had more than one author. First, there are clear evidences of differing writing styles. One need not go far beyond the Prologue to see that the intense, heightened poetry will not be sustained throughout the gospel. Brown as well notes several unique terms in this section.[44] Chapter twenty-one, the second ending to the gospel, also differs in style.

---

44 Brown, Raymond E. Introduction; *The Gospel according to John I-XII*, *The Anchor Bible, v. 29*. (Doubleday and Company, Inc., Garden City, New York, 1966.)

A number of the narratives abruptly break from one scene to another. Some sequences are inconsistent. At the last supper, we read, in John 14: 31, "Rise, let us go from here." But, instead of rising and going, Jesus is presented as giving his discourse on the true vine (chapter fifteen), the prediction of being excommunicated from the synagogues and eventual triumph (chapter sixteen), and his priestly prayer (chapter seventeen). Then they rise and go.

In chapter 20: 30-31, we read, "Now Jesus did many other signs in the presence of the disciples, which are not written in this book; but these are written so that you may believe that Jesus is the Christ, the Son of God, and that by believing you may have life in his name." This certainly sounds like a conclusion, but it is followed by another chapter (inconsistent in style, as noted above) with another conclusion.

John the Baptist testified to his disciples that Jesus was the Son of God in 1: 29-34. Yet, in 3: 26-30, John's disciple seem to know nothing of what John said in chapter one.

In 13: 36, Peter asks where Jesus, who had spoken elliptically about going somewhere, was going. In 14: 5, Thomas indirectly asks where Jesus is going. Yet in 16: 5, Jesus asserts that no one has asked him where he is going.

Another problem is the repetitions and passages which are out of context in the discourses. Brown sees 5: 26-30 as a repetition of 5: 19-25, each deriving from a separate tradition. Likewise the bread of life discourse in 6: 51-58 is almost the same as that in 6: 35-50. The last discourse in 14: 1-31 is largely repeated in 16: 4-33. All of these examples suggest that there were two sources for each discourse, and the evangelist or a redactor did not want a tradition to be lost.

One last illustration of the problems with order occurs in chapter twelve. In 12: 36, we learn that Jesus departed and hid himself. After a brief essay by the evangelist on the unbelief of the people, Jesus cries out and tells his hearers that he has come to save them (12: 44-50). It would seem likely that the discourse closing the chapter was given before Jesus departed and hid himself, or was given in another context altogether.

Modern scholars have put forth three possible solutions to the issues outlined above. These are Accidental Displacement, Multiple Sources, and Multiple Editions. Each possible solution has a range of variability depending upon the approach of the scholar. For example, one scholar may see material accidentally displaced in many places throughout the gospel, while another sees only one or two instances. Also, solutions may be combined, multiple sources seeming to solve a problem here, accidental displacement solving a problem there, and so forth.

Tatian (about 175) was one of the first to re-order the gospel of John for its inclusion into his Diatesseron, a compilation of all four gospels into a single narrative. This kind of activity could result in accidental displacement, based upon the understanding or misunderstanding of the redactor. This points out one of the principle objections to the accidental displacement theory, namely, that the rearrangement reflects the purposes of the redactor rather than the purposes of the evangelist. Another objection is the difficulty in accidentally moving one section to another location. Exactly how could this be done accidentally? Further, since there is no other text, there is no evidence of another order unless the gospel were accidentally rearranged before it was published. Finally, the rearrangement would have had to occur after the death of the evangelist, because he would have been, presumably, in a position to restore the original order.

The combination of several sources can explain stylistic differences, the duplications, and breaks in sequence. That seems to solve a number of problems, but, again, the devil is in the details. Did the evangelist compose any of the gospel, or is it entirely derived from received sources? Were the sources written, oral, or both? Did one or more redactors add material which the evangelist omitted from a source used by the evangelist, or from an entirely different source? How many sources were used, and how can we differentiate them? To the extent that much of the gospel is stylistically consistent, the multiple source theory is compromised.

Those who posit multiple editions suggest that the evangelist's work has been redacted one or more times before it was widely published. One theory suggests a radical rewrite of the original formulation. Given the general homogeneity of style in the gospel, if there had been an extensive rewrite, it must have come from the evangelist himself. Then, one or more redactors, not wanting to lose traditional material in his possession, broke sequences, introduced repetitions and stylistic differences, and disrupted the original order out of devotion to his material.

The composition tentatively proposed by Raymond Brown sees a long period of development over five stages. First, he posits authentic traditional material which is independent of the sources of the synoptic gospels, Matthew, Mark, and Luke, whose gospels will be discussed in the next chapter. Brown, like many scholars, believes there grew up a Johannine "school" where like minded followers of the Apostle John, at first under his guidance, developed their thoughts and teachings into their unique kerygma. The second stage of development required several decades as their teaching and preaching developed into some specific units of the gospel. The third stage resulted in the first edition of the gospel when someone, probably a disciple of the Apostle and the leader of the school, put the units together into a whole narrative. Brown designates this anonymous person as the evangelist. (The Johannine school survived for several more decades, probably producing the epistles ascribed to the Apostle.) Brown thinks that the evangelist survived long enough to edit the gospel again to account for current problems, perhaps especially, the expulsion of Palestinian Christians from the synagogues. This edit, if it were by the evangelist, would be consistent in style with the first edition of the gospel, although the theology of the first edition had probably developed, perhaps considerably in some dimensions. The fifth stage is seen as a final editing of the gospel by a disciple of the evangelist, the third generation of the Johannine school. Brown thinks it likely that this edit included all of the other surviving stage two material, accounting for some of the breaks and repetitions in the gospel.

In addition to the economy evident in the process, this tentative theory solves many problems Brown pointed out in the previous discussion. A tradition separate from the synoptic tradition, especially a separate Palestinian tradition, obviously fits well with the historical context of the birth and early years of Christianity. The source of the tradition may well be John the Apostle. As John preached through several communities, he was likely developing his own stage one traditions. A disciple would have been responsible for stages two through four, and a redactor for stage five.

Brown dates the gospel to the years 75 to 110. The final edition could not have been published before the excommunication of Christians and the development of early sacramentalism in the church, but the presumed first edition could date to 75 to 85, contemporaneous with the development of the Gospel of Matthew.

Key Points

- Stylistic differences, repetitions, breaks in sequence, and inconsistencies strongly argue against a single author for the gospel.
- Three possible solutions, accidental displacement, multiple sources, and multiple editions, have been proposed.
- Raymond Brown blends the latter two theories into a theory of extended development over decades, holding:
    o An original, authentic Palestinian tradition, possibly beginning with the Apostle John.
    o Development, over time through teaching and preaching, into narratives.
    o The anonymous evangelist developed the first edition of the gospel, possibly in 75 – 85.
    o The evangelist redacted his first edition to account for current issues and problems, especially the expulsion of Jewish Christians from the synagogues.
    o Finally, a disciple of the evangelist added ancient material, lest it be lost, to produce the final gospel, 90-110.

Copies of Copies of Copies

When Lodovico Antonio Muratori discovered the canon of scripture which now bears his name, he was appalled by his discovery. The canon was part of a larger manuscript which Muratori published in 1740. Not only was the Latin in which the manuscript was written "truly awful," but the copyist, in another part of the manuscript, had made a serious mistake: he had copied the same thirty lines twice. Worse yet, the copyist made some thirty errors in copying the same thirty lines.

There are possible explanations for these errors. The poor quality of the Latin might be explained by the time the translation was made, probably in the seventh or eighth century as Latin declined into vernacular languages, or even the place, if Latin was not much used in that place. Copying the same lines more than once may happen when the opening line of a section is familiar. Even the large number of errors can be explained: perhaps the copyist was not a professional copyist, but simply someone who could read and wanted to preserve or pass on information.

That's the problem with copies of copies. There were no churches we know of in the first or early second centuries. Letters and other documents were read to the gathered Christians, who may have been somewhat less literate than the estimated fifteen percent of the population who could read, write, or both. It is likely that these documents were copied by literate Christians who were not professional copyists. It is likely that professional copyists had a small roll in preserving New Testament scriptures until well into the fourth century. The implication is that by then most of the mistakes had already been made.

The oldest New Testament texts we have are written on papyrus. The papyri were glued together into scrolls. The 127 papyri we have (at this moment) are mostly New Testament texts covering just a few verses of one document. They are generally small and date from the second to the seventh centuries, most belonging to the third.

Christians favored the codex or book form to scrolls. Until about the ninth century, texts were lettered by hand in upper case letters (unicals) without punctuation or paragraphing. (You can see what these texts look like by using an internet search engine for either of the codices mentioned below.) There are a large number of early translations into Latin, Syrian and other languages. Some of these may be translations of missing manuscripts, which makes it difficult to evaluate them. The Vulgate was commissioned to bring some order into translations of the bible. Translations take the codex (book) form.

There are six highly prized codices dating from the fourth to the sixth centuries. The Codex Vaticanus and Codex Sinaiticus, both fourth century books which contain the complete New Testament accepted by the churches which sponsored them, are the two most highly prized codices. One analysis reported that there are over three thousand variations in the gospels alone between the Codex Vaticanus and Codex Sinaiticus.[45] Most of these are not material, but it provides one measure of the problem. Scholarly estimates of variances in the entire New Testament range from two hundred thousand to four hundred thousand. Again, most are not material, but some at least sow confusion.

Key Points

- We have no original gospel texts (autographs).
- Textual integrity has been compromised by the process of copying texts. Errors by copyists, especially copyists who are not professional copyists, are inevitable.
- Professional copyists had a minimal role, if any, in the first three plus centuries of Christianity.
- Most copyist errors are not material, but some may be.

Corrections to the Gospel Texts

When a copyist changed Abiathar to Ahimelec in Mark 2: 26, he was doing the evangelist a favor. Ahimelec, the father of Abiathar, was in fact the High Priest when that incident occurred. The change to the text, which may or may not as of that time have been regarded as sacred, was intended to correct an error of fact.

What is a scribe to do? Not change a factual error? What about potential misunderstandings? Does he have an obligation to clarify the text? Even more difficult, how could a scribe not make a correction when just a slight change could avoid a misinterpretation of the evangelist's message? Furthermore, certainly, some thought, one is obliged to clarify

---

45 Hoskier, Herman C. *Codex B and its Allies.* (Bernard Quaritch; London, 1914) as reported in *Wikipedia*, "Comparison of Codices Sinaiticus and Vaticanus."

texts which suggest or support heresy. Did any of these things really happen?

Although this is not a "correction" as we are using the term here, think back to the passage where Jesus was saying that he did not come to abolish the law (Mt 5: 17-19). If that pericope were composed in order to picture Paul as least in the kingdom of heaven, the author must have felt very passionately about his theology in order to put his theology into the mouth of Jesus.

In Mark 15: 34, Mark reports Jesus as crying out, "My God, my God, why have you forsaken me?" Some early Christians were perplexed as to how Jesus could be a divine being and still suffer, as he was obviously suffering on the cross when he uttered those words. One of the theological speculations which attempted to solve this problem distinguished between Jesus the man and Christ the god. This form of Docetism[46] taught that Christ the god entered Jesus the man at Jesus' baptism. Christ stayed with Jesus through his ministry, enabling Jesus' miracles and left Jesus when Jesus was dying on the cross, because God could not suffer. If the copyist were in a place where this form of Docetism was widespread, he might consider changing Jesus' desperate plea of abandonment to "Why have you mocked me?" which is what we read in some texts.

Another change related to Docetism and Adoptionist theology (holding that Jesus is not of the same substance of God, but is an adopted son of God) occurred in Luke's account of the baptism of Jesus (Luke 3: 22). The voice of God at the baptism: "Today I have begotten you," becomes in some manuscripts, "You are my beloved son; with you I am well pleased." In the first, Jesus seems to become God's son at his baptism. In the second, Jesus may be God's pre-existent son. That is a huge difference in meaning.

In Luke's account of the presentation of Jesus to the Temple, his parents were astounded at the praise heaped upon him by Simeon. Luke (2: 33) says "And his father and his mother marveled at what was said about him." Some manuscripts were changed to "Joseph and his mother

---

46 Docetism is derived from a verb meaning to appear. It attempts to resolve the problem of the person of Jesus Christ by asserting that he merely appeared to be human. In one form of Docetism, the divine Jesus was not crucified, but a stand in, another human being, which might explain the different text.

marveled…" apparently to combat Adoptionism. The son of Joseph and Mary could not be the son of God except by adoption.

One more example of a theology directed change occurs in Luke 2: 48, where Joseph and Mary find Jesus in the Temple amazing the Temple teachers. "Behold, your father and I have been searching for you in great distress," becomes, "We have been anxiously looking for you," leaving the paternity of Jesus ambiguous.

In chapter twenty-four of Matthew, Jesus is talking about the apocalyptic events about to destroy the age. Just after the parable of the fig tree, verse 36 says, "But concerning that day and hour no one knows, not even the angels of heaven, nor the Son, but the Father only." Some manuscripts omit the words, "nor the Son." Was this an accident or an attempt to prevent the reader from misinterpreting the evangelist's message?

What has been discussed above are thought to be deliberate changes, most of which may have been made to promote a particular theological position. Most of the deliberate theological changes were made in second and third centuries, before a consensus formed on the canon of scripture. These theological battles were vigorously fought during these times, and these changes may be evidence of these struggles.

As for the well-meaning scribe who fixed the reference to the High Priest in Mark 2: 26, in most English translations you will find the original reference to Abiathar. The translators justify the retention of Abiathar on the grounds that the setting was in the days of Abiathar, not in the high priesthood of Abiathar.

But there is another class of errors, simple mistakes. The most common of these would be simply confusing one word with another. It is surprisingly easy, relatively speaking, to skip a word, or even a line or a verse when that line or verse ends with the same word. Remember the lesson of the copyist discovered by Muratori: some thirty mistakes in thirty lines, having copied the same thirty lines by mistake.

Accidental changes far outnumber the deliberate changes. Furthermore, accidental changes are usually not very important and can often be recognized. That said, the large number of accidental changes increases the probability that some changes are important or difficult to unravel.

Key Points

- The vast majority of changes to gospel texts are accidental, and the vast majority of these are not material.
- The deliberate changes to gospel texts are made for high-minded reasons: to correct an error of fact, to prevent a reader from misinterpreting the evangelist's intended meaning, to prevent a misunderstanding, to frustrate "heterodoxy," or to promote "orthodoxy."
- What is now the canon of the New Testament had not yet been accepted by all the churches, although there was wide agreement with respect to the four gospels and the "Pauline" epistles in the third century.

Chapter Six: The Development of the Gospels, Part II

The ABCs of the Synoptic Gospels

This section contains elementary information about the synoptic gospels, the Gospels of Matthew, Mark, and Luke. The literal meaning of "synoptic" is "with the eye." It is an apt description of these three gospels because, when these gospels are arranged side by side as in any Harmony of the gospels, it is immediately apparent that these gospels are very similar, yet somewhat different.

The traditional order of the gospels is Matthew, Mark, Luke, and John. One of the first witnesses to that order is Irenaeus (writing about 180). Irenaeus named all four canonical gospels and quoted from them. Furthermore, he claimed with authority that there were four and only four canonical gospels because there were only four zones in the world, four principle winds, and four principle directions. Irenaeus wrote that Matthew was written in Hebrew while Peter and Paul were preaching in Rome, that is, in the sixties. Paul is believed to have been beheaded under the Neronian persecution in 64, but certainly no later than 67. Irenaeus goes on to say that Mark was written shortly after Matthew was written. Irenaeus is joined by many other church fathers in labeling Matthew as the first gospel.

That view prevailed for many centuries. Today, however, few modern scholars accept the priority of Matthew. Furthermore, they see the composition dates assigned by Irenaeus as impossibly early. They rather uniformly reject the proposition that the original Matthew was written either in Hebrew or in Aramaic, the language spoken in Palestine in the time of Christ and for several centuries before.

When Tatian composed his *Diatesseron* (about 175), a single narrative composed from all four gospels, he did so in part because he recognized the considerable amount of duplication in the gospels. However, it wasn't until the eighteenth, nineteenth, and twentieth centuries that the duplications were studied in detail. The results of these studies are still argued today. What follows is a simple explication of mainstream, but certainly not universal, scholarly thinking about the synoptic gospels.

The first gospel composed was that attributed to Mark. It was composed during the years of the revolt (66–73) against Rome which ended with the destruction of the Temple by Titus in 70 and the Roman victory at Masada in 73. Since chapter thirteen of Mark contains a prediction of the destruction of the Temple, many, but not all, are persuaded that the earliest date of composition must be 70, and likely a year or two later.

The Markan account is the story of Jesus the miracle worker. The gospel seems to be a series of pericopes strung together with connectives plus an account of the passion, which extends to more than one-third of the gospel. (One author described the composition of Mark as the evangelist supplying the string for the pearls of the pericopes.) It is assumed that the pericopes pre-existed the evangelist, but that may not be true in every single case.

Some scholars see Mark's gospel as divisible into two parts. Part I portrays the Galilean ministry, ending with 8: 29. It is largely a fast paced story of a miracle worker moving swiftly from place to place to evangelize. Chapter 8: 30 begins Part II, which contains far more narrative than Part I. The previous theme of Jesus the miracle worker is shaded into predictions of suffering and death, talk of persecution, and a prediction of the end of the world we know.

Some authors suggest that the Markan passion narrative is conflated by Mark with the insertion of such material as the agony in Gethsemane, the cutting of the servant's ear during the arrest of Jesus, the extended account of Jesus before the Sanhedrin, and several other details.[47] The result of stripping out the Markan conflations is a primitive account of

---

47   See Jeremias, Joachim. *The Eucharistic Words of Jesus.* P. 89-96.

the passion, perhaps the first written narrative about Jesus. It has been argued that the evangelist of John also relied on this primitive account for his passion narrative.

Scholars converge on the priority of Mark for a number of reasons. The shortest gospel is that of Mark. Over eighty percent of the gospel of Mark is contained in the gospel of Matthew, and at least fifty percent of Mark is contained in Luke. Moreover, Matthew and Luke have some 200 verses in common with each other which are not found in Mark, suggesting another source document, one which was not available to Mark.

The vocabulary of Mark is not the stylish Greek of Luke, or even as good as that of Matthew. Mark's gospel is marked by many semiticisms which more careful writers would have cleaned up. In fact, both Matthew and Luke changed Mark's rough vocabulary in a number of places to proper Greek, offering testimony to Mark's priority.

A similar argument is made from the so-called harder readings. These are places where the directness of Mark's words might give offense to some readers. Here is just one example. We read in Mark 6: 5, concerning Jesus' visit to Nazareth, "And he could do no mighty work there…" When Matthew describes the same visit in 13: 58, he tones down Mark's statement: "And he did not do many mighty works there, because of their unbelief." Luke does not mention this incident. The characteristic style of Mark is mitigated by the more refined writing of Matthew and Luke, suggesting Markan priority.

The order of the narratives in Mark seems to have been followed, more or less, by the succeeding synoptics. When there has been some rearrangement of material, scholars have found reasons to prefer Mark's order.

We will discuss the theology of the gospels below, but it is enough to say here that the theology in Mark's gospel is less developed than the theology in either Matthew or Luke, arguing for an earlier date.

Since the gospels of Matthew and Luke seem to be independent of one another—material found only in one gospel is not, obviously, found in the other—dating is more difficult. Most scholars favor early dating for these gospels, possibly the 70s to 80s for Matthew and 80s to 90s for Luke.

Matthew and Luke do share material, but that material is assumed to derive from another source used by both evangelists, the Q document. One reason a separate written source is hypothecated—no written evidence of such a document has emerged yet—is that the two gospels use the source in markedly different ways, and yet, there is a very high degree of conformity between the pericopes used by each evangelist. The high degree of uniformity argues for a written source, while the individualistic use of the material suggests that Matthew and Luke did not know each other.

We are accustomed to having all four gospels available. That was not the case in the first and second centuries. The gospels were not developed by the first generation of Christians, but by the second and third generations. Furthermore, individual congregations generally had a favorite gospel which they used, often to the exclusion of other gospels. Those individual favorites were not limited to the four gospels we today accept as canonical. There was no canon in the first and second centuries (or even in the third and fourth centuries, although there was by that time a high degree of consensus, especially as to the gospels and many epistles). Many different gospels, perhaps twenty, were used by various congregations throughout the Empire in the first centuries of the common era. What became the four canonical gospels became known in different places at different times. It is the middle of the second century before we have evidence of all four canonical gospels known in one place, and one place is not every place.[48]

Key Points

- The synoptic gospels are so similar in content that as early as the second century there was an attempt to harmonize them.
- At the same time, there are differences in emphases, theologies, order, and some details.
- A number of theories have been advanced to explain how this similarity and divergence came to be. The two document theory and variations thereof, seem to have the most support among scholars today.

---

48   Reinach, Solomon. *Orpheus.* (Horace Liveright; New York, 1930)

- The first source document is the *Gospel according to Mark*. Mark is rather clearly the first gospel. It is contained almost entirely in Matthew and largely in Luke.
- The second hypothecated source document is Q, a document of narratives used independently by Matthew and Luke. Matthew and Luke share over two hundred verses from this source, but in differing orders. In spite of the differences in order, there is a convincingly high agreement of subject, words, styles, and even parenthetical expressions between Matthew and Luke to demonstrate a common written source.
- Both Matthew and Luke had access to additional traditional material, written, oral or both. However, it does not appear that Matthew knew Luke, or that Luke knew Matthew.
- Some scholars argue for a third source, or a third and a fourth source.

The Theologies of the Gospels

A major issue when discussing a theology of a gospel or epistle is the danger of projecting what the viewer wants to see into the document. It is relatively easy to cite passages, some fairly clear, some ambivalent, and to build a case for one's theology which seems reinforced by a multitude of citations. This is an especial problem when the reader has fully embraced a particular point of view; then, the seeker is not even aware of his mental selection. Letting the document speak for itself is surprisingly difficult, and, it may lead to another problem. There may be contradictions or confusion within the document itself, especially if, like the gospels, there have been one or more redactions. Clearly, there is room for a variety of opinions regarding theology.

The discussions below are gathered from a variety of sources, each of which is deemed reliable.[49] There are differences among the sources,

---

49 Reliable here means that the source is qualified by education and experience to

and the final summary below is the responsibility of the author, even though the author has contributed no new ideas to the discussion. No attempt has been made to identify a particular strain of thought because, usually, there are a number of thinkers with similar or complementary positions, albeit sometimes with small permutations not cited here.

The Theology of Mark's Gospel

One knows immediately, at least in part, what Mark is about. "The beginning of the gospel of Jesus Christ, the Son of God." (Mark 1: 1) Jesus is the Christ and the Son of God. The Messiaship of Jesus may be markedly different from the expectations of contemporary Jews, but Mark affirms Jesus as Messiah, and more, Son of God. One can argue over the nature of Jesus' sonship, pre-existent or adoptive, but the language of 1: 11—"You are my beloved Son; with you I am well pleased"—can be interpreted to favor either one. Other text variations are more clearly Adoptionist.

This opening statement is incredible except in light of the resurrection of Jesus. Mark's good news depends upon the resurrection, as the gospel itself shows below. The Jesus of Mark is a miracle worker who died for our sins. The proof of his mission and its acceptance by God is his resurrection from the dead.

Mark establishes John the Baptist as the fulfillment of Isaiah's sentence regarding a messenger to prepare the way. John baptizes Jesus, which occasions the "heavens being torn open and the Spirit descending on him like a dove." (Mark 1: 10)

This is a profound statement in eleven verses. Even more, upon reflection and understanding the message of the rest of the gospel, the Messiaship of Jesus does not rest on the antecedent of the chosen people. There is no attempt to prove Jesus was of the house of David. Salvation history begins with Jesus' baptism by John the Baptist. There are no other antecedents. Furthermore, Mark's order of salvation history is followed by the other evangelists.[50] John the Baptist is mentioned in

---

offer an opinion on the subject, has published one or more opinions, and has been critiqued by scholars similarly qualified.

50   Luke relates the incident called the Presentation and the time when Jesus was

the prologue of the gospel of John, although there is no baptism of Jesus narrative.

Israel is not the womb of the Christian experience. Mark's gospel demonstrates little precision with things Jewish, reinforcing its generally accepted gentile provenance. Furthermore, the gospel shows a growing alienation from Judaism. The Jews are in opposition to Jesus from the very beginning, but their hostility grows throughout such that "...the chief priests and the Scribes were seeking how to arrest him by stealth and kill him..." (14: 1) It is the Sanhedrin which hands Jesus over to Pilate.

The Jesus portrayed by Mark displays a range of human behaviors. Indignation, fear, sadness, anger, surprise, sympathy, all are on display. He even admits ignorance (13: 32). However, he also has a very strong sense of his mission (for example, 1: 15, 1: 38-39, 8: 31-33, 9: 30-32, 10: 32-34).

The disciples enthusiastically follow Jesus in the beginning of his ministry. Later, they are sometimes uncomprehending (for example, 4: 13, 4: 33-34), sometimes critical, even snide (for example, 5: 31, 6: 37). At the end, they are frightened, cowed and unbelieving (14: 66-72, 15: 40 mentions not one of his twelve most intimate followers, 16: 9-11, 14).

If, as some authors suggest, the disciples are a type—stand-ins—for the Christian congregations, the descent of the disciples may reflect the travails of these churches. Conceived in glory after the resurrection, the congregations are racked by political and theological disputes (the Palestinian congregations against Paul's Greek congregations), and finally (for Mark), meeting persecution and death, witnessing the heroic death of martyrs and the falling away of those who recanted their Christian faith.

The element of secrecy is evident in Mark (for example, 4: 10-12). Jesus tells his disciples not to let others know that he is the Christ. He commands the devils he has exorcised and others who benefited from his miracles not to speak publicly. This element strikes readers as peculiar.

---

discovered teaching in the Temple. These two stories, together with the infancy narratives of Matthew and Luke are not often regarded as the beginning of salvation history because of their legendary character.

One reason for secrecy may be the difference in the concept of the Messiah. Many Jews were looking for a military or political leader who would vanquish their opponents and restore the Jewish state. Jesus knew that was not his role, even though this is the reason for which he was crucified. If his true mission cannot be known except in the light of his resurrection, he must best keep his mission secret. The cost of this secrecy is confusion among the disciples.

Another possible explanation is that secrecy is required because of the faithlessness of the Jews. They couldn't get the message because they were not worthy (very likely an apologetic value judgment) of the secret message (4: 11-12). That also explains, apologetically, the failure of Jesus' mission to the chosen people.

Another possible explanation which may combine elements of both of the above is that the Messiah Jesus can be understood only in the light of his resurrection. His life, his message, his suffering make no sense if he is not resurrected. Good Pauline theology.

It would be blind to fail to note the apocalypticism of chapter thirteen. Were it not for the presence of verse 30, the end of days could be read as a future event.

Key Points

- There is a variety of opinions as to the theology presented in the Gospel of Mark. The following points may be in dispute among theologians. They are, however, taken from reliable sources, even though these reliable sources at times may disagree with one another.
- Jesus is the Christ, but he is not the Messiah expected by the Jews. Jesus' Messiaship can be understood only in light of his resurrection from the dead.
- Salvation history begins with John baptizing Jesus. Jesus was a Jew, and according to Christian evangelists, Jewish prophets foretold his Messiaship. However, Jews in general, unlike Mark, did not look to the suffering servant in deutero-Isaiah[51] as their Messiah. In Mark

---

51 For many centuries, the book of Isaiah was believed to be the product of one

there is no effort to connect Jesus to the royal family of David.

- The behavior of Jesus as portrayed by Mark is distinctly and comprehensively human, except, of course, for his many miracles.
- Mark's Jesus had a clear sense of mission.
- The attitudes of the disciples may reflect the actual conditions of the Christian congregations during the lifetime of Mark.
- The element of secrecy in Mark may be best explained by the behavior of the disciples: they understood little until they witnessed the resurrection of Jesus.
- "Truly, I say to you, this generation will not pass away until all these things take place." Mark 13: 30, regarding the apocalypse.

The Theology of Matthew's Gospel

If the Gospel of Mark is a string of barely related pericopes, the Gospel of Matthew is composed with much greater craft. Many scholars see five major discourses, each preceded by miracles or other stories, and these five discourses are bracketed between an introduction and a conclusion.

The introductory material includes the genealogy of Joseph, the birth of Jesus, the visit of the Wise Men, and the flight into Egypt, chapters one and two. It should be noted here that Matthew attests to the virgin birth, and an angel informs Joseph that Jesus will save his people from their sins. The reason for tracing Joseph to the House of David is unclear if Joseph is not the father of Jesus.

Chapters three and four contain the pericopes which introduce the first discourse. These are the baptism of Jesus narrative, which follows that of Mark, and the temptation in the desert narrative, which follows

person, Isaiah. Beginning in the nineteenth century, some authors proposed that chapters 40 through 55 were written by another hand. Their basis was the distinctive style of these chapters as opposed to the style of the preceding and subsequent chapters, and the change in subject matter and tone. Subsequently, some authors have proposed a third hand for chapters 56 to 66.

immediately after the baptism story, as in Mark's gospel. The first discourse, the sermon on the mount, includes chapters five through seven. Chapters eight and nine contain mainly healing stories. Chapter ten contains the second discourse, the missionary instructions. In chapters eleven and twelve, there is a variety of stories, including the messengers from John the Baptist, a sabbath controversy, and closing with Jesus defining his family as those who do the will of his Father in heaven. The third discourse is a collection of parables, chapter thirteen. Chapters fourteen through seventeen contain a variety of narratives starting with the death of John the Baptist and ending with the transfiguration and the Temple tax. The fourth discourse is a sermon on humility and forgiveness in chapter eighteen. Another series of diverse narratives in chapters nineteen through twenty-two introduce the fifth discourse, the eschatological sermon in chapters twenty-three through twenty-five.

The passion and resurrection, chapters twenty-six through twenty-eight, provide the conclusion to the gospel.

The evangelist is very likely a Palestinian Christian. He knows the practices of the Jews, and he cites connections between Jewish scripture and his portrayal of Jesus far more than Mark and Luke. The five-fold construction of his gospel may be intended to recall the five books of Moses. The Jesus Matthew presents is like Moses, a teacher and lawgiver.

The gospel lacks any vivid descriptions, personal memories, or first person expressions which one might expect from an eyewitness like the Apostle Matthew. As mentioned previously, almost all of Mark is contained in Matthew. Matthew does not correct Mark's account. Thus, we may conclude that Matthew is further removed from the events he reports than Mark, who was not himself an eyewitness.

Much of the rest of Matthew is derived from another written source, Q. It is inconceivable that an eyewitness would depend so thoroughly on documentary sources.

Theologians have written volumes on the various titles the evangelists apply to Jesus. In short, we have found no persuasive consensus as to the meaning of "Son of Man," and the title, "Son of God" is repeatedly compromised by textual ambiguities, especially including differences in the Greek texts themselves, as to whether it means pre-existent sonship or Adoptionist sonship. (Many theologians on both sides of the argument would disagree with that statement.)

Matthew seems to be of two minds regarding his Jewish religion. He has Jesus urging his hearers to observe the teachings of the Scribes and the Pharisees in 23: 2-3. In 17: 27, Jesus is concerned not to give offense to a tax collector. But on five occasions Matthew speaks of their synagogues, as if the split between Palestinian Christians and Jews had already occurred.[52]

The bulk of chapter 23 is a harsh recitation of the coming woes of the Scribes and Pharisees, and 27: 25 shows clearly the schism and can be seen to have given up hope for the Christian mission to the Jews.

If the Jews are unworthy of the good news, then the gospel must be preached throughout the world. This, in fact, is Jesus' final command to his disciples in the closing verses of Matthew (28: 16-20).

Again, it would be blind not to note that Matthew has incorporated the apocalypticism of Mark into his gospel, with the same pronouncement that this generation will not pass away before these things occur. (Matthew 24: 34)

Key Points

- The Gospel of Matthew is a carefully wrought expansion of the Gospel of Mark.
- The evangelist is very likely a Palestinian Christian who, unlike Mark, is very familiar with Jewish practices and scriptures. He pictures Jesus as the fulfillment of Jewish scriptures.
- The anonymous evangelist is not an eyewitness to the events he reports. In fact, he relies on pre-existing documents for his narrative.
- It is difficult to escape the conclusion that Matthew was written after the expulsion of the Christians from the synagogues, at least in Palestine, which was probably completed in Palestine around the years 85 to 90.

52   4: 23, 9: 35, 10: 17, 12: 9, 13: 54.

- Although Paul had already preached his gospel to the gentiles, the failure of the Christian mission to the Jews allowed Palestinian Christians to endorse a universal mission to all nations, and, very importantly, not to insist upon observance of the Law.
- Matthew incorporates Mark's apocalypticism into his own gospel.

The Theology of Luke's Gospel

There is a broad consensus that *Acts of the Apostles* and the *Gospel according to Luke* are from the same hand. They appear to be volume one and volume two of a continuous work. Each document may fill a scroll, which may or may not explain the fact of two volumes. The two volumes became more separate when churches adopted the relatively late *Gospel according to John* and inserted it between *Acts* and Luke.

Luke is rather obviously a Greek Christian with a considerably different outlook from Mark and Matthew. While Mark, and Matthew following, both saw the end of time coming soon, Luke is more concerned—he still has the apocalyptic language with the declaration that this generation will not pass away—with what the Christian is to do today, now. In this, he shows Jesus as a friend of the poor, the outcast, even the criminal. By the time he was writing his works, the mission to the Jews had failed, Paul and Peter were dead, and Christians had been excommunicated from the synagogues. Greek congregations no longer had anything to fear from Judaizers. The hope for spreading the good news lay among the gentiles.

Here are some indications of Luke's outlook for spreading the gospel once the Jews had rejected it.

Samaritans, as pointed out earlier, were despised by Jews, even though Samaritans claimed to be Jewish and performed Temple rites on Mount Gerazim. They were so despised that the lawyer testing Jesus cannot use that name to describe the man who proved to be a good neighbor in the parable of the Good Samaritan (10: 25-37). He must resort to a circumlocution. Then Jesus tells him to go and do likewise—to be like a Samaritan.

In chapter seventeen, Jesus cleanses ten lepers of their illness. One, a Samaritan, returns to thank Jesus for the grace of his cure. As Jesus asks about the other nine, he labels this man a foreigner, which may be the least opprobrious, but still opprobrious epithet a Jew would use to describe a Samaritan. Luke seems to say that the missionary field is the whole world, if it includes even Samaritans. This cure, like the parable of the Good Samaritan, is unique to Luke.

Finally, in *Acts* 8: 4-25 Philip evangelizes in Samaria with considerable success.

The focus of the genealogy of Joseph in Luke is different from that of Matthew. Luke admits to tracing Joseph to the Davidic line, but he does not go back to Abraham, the supposed father of the Jews. He goes back to Adam, the supposed father of all mankind. Again, the reason for tracing Joseph to the House of David is unclear if Joseph is not the father of Jesus.

Is Luke transmitting fragments of liturgy in the first two chapters, which contain three canticles, the Magnificat (1: 46-55), the Benedictus, (1: 68-79), and the Nunc Dimittis (2: 29-32)? The common opinion derives the liturgy from this gospel, but, again, this is purely Lukan material, at least opening the possibility of another source available only to Luke. If so, this source would have been a theologically developed source from, rather than to, the liturgy.

A current controversy among theologians is the theology of atonement in Luke, specifically, is there a theology of atonement. A number of scholars have noted, having impeached the authority of certain texts (Lk 22: 19-20, Acts 20: 28), that Luke does not picture Christ's death as redemptive. They argue that it is Christ's exaltation and the coming of the Holy Spirit which turn the world to God. Others are content to accept the texts cited and to refer to the metaphor of the paschal lamb as evidence of the expiatory nature of Christ's death. A further subject of dispute is whether the theology of atonement is Luke's or Paul's.

The Holy Spirit is very active in Luke's writings. For example, the Spirit is active three times in the first chapters alone in connection with the canticles mentioned above. There is no doubt that the exaltation of Jesus and the coming of the Holy Spirit together are central to Luke's theology of salvation. This, however, for a supposed companion of Paul is far from Paul's gospel of faith in the redemptive death of Jesus. But then again, we know that Luke, the companion of Paul, was not the author of this gospel.

Another curiosity about the relationship of Luke to Paul is the very great difference in Paul's travels, as reported in Galatians, and as reported by Luke in *Acts*.

A third curiosity is the three long speeches of Paul reported in *Acts*.[53] Are these Paul's speeches or Luke's? They seem to be something of an apology for the Jewish origins of Christianity. This would be desirable if Palestinian Christians (and Jewish Christians in the diaspora) were perplexed by their expulsion from the synagogues. The defense of the Jewish origins of Christianity contained in these speeches might help Jewish Christians overcome their antipathy to Paul, whom many hard line Jewish Christians regarded as the father of all heresies, and to join Greek congregations rather than to lapse back to Judaism.

The seventh chapter of Luke contains a series of pericopes which present a picture of Jesus at work. First there is the centurion who believes that Jesus can heal his servant from a distance. Then he travels to the village of Nain where he restores to life the son of a widow, possibly her sole support and only hope for the future in this patriarchal society. The messengers from John the Baptist follow, and Jesus gives evidence of his mission. At dinner in the house of a Pharisee, he forgives the sins of a woman who bathes his feet with her tears of repentance.

Luke portrays the person of Jesus through these stories as using his power to help rather ordinary people. He is kind, sympathetic, committed to his mission, and has extraordinary powers extending even to the forgiveness of sins.

Key Points

- Luke's Gospel and *Acts of the Apostles* were composed by the same anonymous author.
- There are a number of pericopes in *Acts* which appear to have a theological purpose: the injunction to the

---

53   *Acts* 13: 16-41, 24: 10-21, and 26: 2-23.

Apostles to remain in Jerusalem until the Spirit comes; the forty day post-resurrection period of sightings of Jesus and the exaltation of Jesus on the fortieth day; the Spirit-filled Apostles preaching to men of all nations and being understood.

- Luke looks to the whole world as the object of the gospel.
    - o The Jews have proved unworthy.
    - o Yet, Luke is carful in *Acts* to ease the transition of the Jewish Christian sects into the new faith, Christianity.
- The Jesus Christ of Luke is a sympathetic human being doing powerful good—even forgiving sin—as he carries out the mission of his Father in heaven.

The Theology of John's Gospel

Over ninety percent of the *Gospel according to John* is original to that gospel. The differences between the gospel of John and the synoptic gospels slap the reader in the face. The Jesus of John is mystical and abstract, ever sure of himself and his mission. How different from the Jesus of Luke, or Mark or Matthew. Even the prologue proclaims his divinity (or emanation). There is no virgin birth, but there is an incarnation: the Word becomes flesh. He often speaks of his heavenly Father and acknowledges his role as savior. John the Baptist gives several testimonies as to Jesus' mission, but none is more economical and descriptive as, "Behold the lamb of God, who takes away the sins of the world." (1: 29) There is no messianic secret here. Unless one interprets Jesus as a Gnostic aeon, he even claims to be one with the Father. He does not usually dispute the charges of his opponents, "the Jews," which term comes across as an often used invective, when they charge him with blasphemy for making himself equal to God. Even when he meets death on the cross, he is in charge, pronouncing the finish of his mission from the cross.

John's gospel lacks many parables, the vignettes which populate the synoptics. John fills his gospel with discourses. The length of Jesus' ministry in John is about three years as opposed to about one year in the synoptics. Judea is the primary location of the ministry in John, while the synoptics keep Jesus in Galilee until his last Passover. John places the Temple cleansing at the beginning of the ministry, while the synoptics place it at the end of his ministry. Although John the Baptist is part of the prologue to the gospel, the narrative of Jesus' baptism, recited in all the synoptics, is missing in John.[54] The last supper, the final meal in John mentioned in 13: 1-2, contrary to the synoptics, is not a Passover meal.

The New Testament gives four accounts of the institution of the eucharist, but John has not one of them. Yet, there is a discourse (6: 27-58) in which Jesus claims to be the bread of life. Even his disciples must have found it hard when he said, "Truly, truly, I say to you, unless you eat the flesh of the Son of Man and drink his blood, you have no life in you. Whoever feeds on my flesh and drinks my blood has eternal life, and I will raise him up on the last day." (6: 53-54) Clearly, one cannot interpret John literally, as, perhaps, some Romans did.

A decent summary of John's theology can be found in 3: 16-21, "For God so loved the world…" It contains the requirement of belief in the Son, eternal life contingent upon belief, the salvific mission of the Son, the centrality of faith in the Son, and the theme of light (good) and darkness (evil).

Around the middle of the twentieth century, a recently developed idea, "realized eschatology," was gaining fashion, especially as a key to understanding the fourth gospel but applicable to the New Testament as a whole. It is a difficult idea to grasp because there are certain understandings which precede the idea. Its development may be seen as part of "Higher Criticism," a largely twentieth century movement which studies the dates, origins, sources and structures of biblical documents in order to understand the genuine meanings of the intended messages, not simply the words themselves.

One postulate of higher criticism is that the notion of "history" is generally (but not always) inapplicable to religious documents. Religious writings are to be understood as ranging from mythological, for example,

---

54 John 1: 32-33 contains the Baptist's witness as to the Spirit descending and remaining upon Jesus, but the circumstances are not completely clear.

most, if not all of Genesis, to the proximately historical, as many of the events reported about Jesus and reported by Paul about Paul. Even in the latter groups, there are likely to be found events which are not, strictly speaking from our contemporary point of view, historical.

With that background, a new attempt was made to understand the words "in a little while," " soon," "at hand," "quickly" as applied in the New Testament to the apocalyptic events prominently mentioned there. The common meanings of those words in their contexts led to the expectation of proximate future eschatological events, the parousia and the end of the world as we know it. But, after all, by mid-twentieth century some two thousand years had passed.

The understanding of future eschatological events arises from the commonly accepted definitions of those words cited above. Realized eschatology notes the religious nature of the writings and attempts to understand the underlying message of those words which seem to promise future events. According to the new interpretation, the words of the New Testament were not wrong or untruthful, but the common understanding of those words in the context of a religious document is wrong. Instead of looking for a proximate future eschatological event, we are to understand that all around us now we see the Kingdom of God on earth, that the Kingdom is now realized or effected or produced by the life, death, and resurrection of Jesus. Jesus has come once and will not come again. We are living in his kingdom. This is the meaning of the many times, in slightly different forms, the Jesus in the gospel of John proclaims that whoever sees him sees the Father, and whoever hears his word and believes has eternal life. The emphasis is on the present, not the future.

Key Points

- The gospel of John is highly original in both content and style.
- Jesus affirms his pre-existence with the Father and looks forward to his return to the Father.
- Jesus is the savior of the world with the power, from the Father, to judge the world and to heal and to forgive sin.

- In summary, John's theology contains the requirement of belief in the Son, eternal life contingent upon belief, the salvific mission of the Son, the centrality of faith in the Son, and the dualistic theme of light (good) and darkness (evil).

- The theology in the *Gospel according to John* is clearly more developed than the theology in the gospel of Luke. The theology in the gospel of Luke is clearly more developed than the theology in the gospel of Matthew. The same can be said of Matthew with respect to Mark. Theology takes reflection, and reflection takes time. Judging from theology alone, the priority of the gospels is established.

- An attempt to understand why Jesus has not returned led to the development of the notion of realized eschatology, that the Kingdom of God is effected in the life, death and resurrection of Jesus. We are not to look for the parousia, or the thousand year reign of Jesus on earth while he brings his enemies to his feet, or to the Rapture.

Chapter Seven: Higher Criticism

Introduction

In the previous chapter we noted the development of the hypothesis of realized eschatology under the rubric of higher criticism. Higher criticism studies the dates, origins, sources and structures of biblical (or other) documents in order to understand the genuine meanings of the intended messages, not simply the words themselves. This discipline implies that the words alone may give an incomplete or even misleading message.

Higher criticism is an historical term which originally was intended to distinguish it from lower criticism. That term, lower criticism, is not often used today, having been replaced by the term textual criticism. There is nothing low or otherwise unworthy in trying to establish the original text of a document. Higher criticism depends on lower or textual criticism. There is today a tendency to replace the term higher criticism with the term historical criticism.

Textual criticism is exactly what it appears to be, an effort to get back to the most accurate texts of the scriptures (or other writings). (Examples of textual criticism were given in chapter six.) It seeks to eliminate scribal errors and to identify the activity of redactors as opposed to authors, among other things. Hort and Wescott published an edition of the New Testament in Greek in 1881 after twenty-eight years of study. Theirs was not the first critical edition, but it was considered the best for many, many years.

Higher criticism distinguished itself from textual criticism by using critical texts to find the meaning behind the words. Various authors assign the beginning of higher criticism to various times. The extreme starting point could be Baruch Spinoza. In his *Tractatus*, published in 1670, he denied that Moses was the author of the Pentateuch and proposed a date of composition during and after return from the exile, an hypothesis held by many today.

In 1753, Jean Astruc sought to defend the authorship of Moses for the Pentateuch by analyzing the Pentateuch in detail to discover the traditions which underlay the texts. He found such traditions and proposed that Moses had cobbled them together into the document we have today. His work, *Conjectures on the original documents that Moses appears to have used in composing the Book of Genesis. With remarks that support or throw light upon these conjectures.* was published anonymously, but it gained him the title of the father of documentary hypotheses.

An expert in oriental languages, Johann Gottfried Eichhorn, in 1870 published his *Introduction to the Old Testament.* His exegesis of the Hebrew Bible concluded that most of the writings of the Hebrew Bible exhibited several authors or redactors. As a modern rationalist, he dismissed all the supernatural events related in the First and New Testaments. When placed in the historical context of the ancient world, he expected to read about miracles, but he believed these wonders were in fact explicable on natural principles. His interest in biblical books was limited to the light they cast upon antiquity.

There are a number of disciplines within the overall rubric of historical criticism. There is overlap, and no one tool is adequate to a thorough study. In virtually all of the disciplines, however, there are two questions which must be answered: what does this pericope mean in the life of Jesus at the time and place depicted in the pericope, and what does this pericope mean in the situation of the contemporary believing community. The following thumbnail sketch will be illustrated later in the chapter.

- Source criticism or literary criticism studies the various types of literary forms, poem, proclamation story, and so forth, seeking to establish the structure, date, and authorship of the pericope.
- Form criticism analyzes the form or structure of documents in order to determine its original form in its

historical context. This may involve trying to trace the oral tradition behind the form being studied.

- Redaction criticism starts with the finished product and then attempts to peel off the latest additions in order to arrive at the primitive form of the pericope. There is an attempt to explain each addition, that is, to determine what each author or redactor had in mind when he made a specific change.
- Tradition criticism attempts to trace the development of pericopes from stage to stage, especially how the oral stage came to be written. It seeks to identify growth in the oral stages of development as well as in the written stages.
- Historical criticism places the document in its historical setting and interprets it in light of its contemporary environment.

It should be obvious from the thumbnail sketch that there is plenty of room for scholars to go astray, to let their imaginations carry them off, and to find what they are seeking. On the other hand, higher criticism has elucidated many, many narratives whose meaning would otherwise never have been clear. The goal of higher criticism is to establish the true meaning of scripture, the original message, the text's primitive meaning in its original historical context and its literal sense. It is clear that these critics believe that the words of scripture often do not convey that message, that scripture is often unhistorical and needs to be cleansed of the theological reflections which have grown into the texts.

Key Points

- Higher criticism studies the dates, origins, sources and structures of biblical (or other) documents in order to understand the genuine meanings of the intended messages, not simply the words themselves.
- By implication, the words themselves do not adequately convey these meanings.

- The methods used by practitioners of higher criticism may appear "fast and loose" to the layperson, but these scholars are disciplined in method and must always contend with the learned opinions of other scholars.

Some Fruits of Higher Criticism

We have mentioned in passing Spinoza's dating of the Pentateuch. It is commonly thought today that the Torah was a product of the Babylonian Captivity. Some of its traditions may go back several centuries, but much of the five books date from the exilic era. Obviously, Moses could not be the author of the Law inasmuch as it was created centuries after his presumed existence.

When Jean Astruc, seeking to defend Moses' authorship, proposed the theory of pre-existing documents, he (eventually) lost his argument but gained everlasting fame as the father of documentary hypotheses.

Eichhorn may be regarded as the father of radical critics, and that back in 1870.

We will not mention at all the contributions of many influential writers such as David F. Strauss (1808 – 1874) who wrote an important "Life of Jesus" which dispensed with miracles and the divinity of Jesus, to the scandal of almost everyone, as did Ernst Renan (1823 -1892), whose Life of Jesus may still be in print. Instead, we will proceed to discuss airily some chains of stories and then to illustrate in a little more depth the application of some techniques in the work of specific authors.

Chains of Stories

After the first great discourse in Matthew, the sermon on the mount, there is a series of ten miracle stories, mostly healings, interrupted here and there by other pericopes. In the first, Jesus heals a leper and enjoins him to keep silent. Matthew omits the healed man's talking about the cure which is found in the parallel passage in Mark 1: 40-45.

There follows the story of the cure of the centurion's servant from a distance. Matthew uses the centurion's faith in Jesus' power to excoriate the lack of faith among the Jews and to lead into the second great discourse, the missionary commission, for "...many will come from east and west and recline at table with Abraham, Isaac, and Jacob in the kingdom of heaven, while the sons of the kingdom will be thrown into the outer darkness." (Matthew 8: 11-12) The faith of this pagan exceeded that of Jesus' countrymen, the Jews. The following missionary commission invites pagans to replace Jews as the new "chosen people." This story, read together with the following discourse, reflects the crisis in the situation in the Christian communities in Palestine. Relationships with Jews in the synagogue were becoming increasingly strained. It is probable that by the time of the appearance of the *Gospel according to Matthew* Christians were being or had been expelled from the synagogues. The miracle story validates the mission of Jesus and the faith of the Christians. The meaning of the story uncovered by historical criticism suggests the failure of the Christian mission to the Jews—the Jews weren't buying it. This reflects the actual situation of the Christian congregations in Palestine at the end of the first century. The message uncovered by historical criticism surpasses the message of the mere words of the text.

After the third miracle, the cure of Simon's mother and many others brought to Jesus, there follow two pronouncement stories. When Jesus was preparing to leave, a scribe declares he will follow Jesus wherever he goes. Jesus replies that foxes have holes and birds have nests, but the Son of Man has nowhere to lay his head. This is followed immediately by a disciple who wants permission to bury his father before following, but Jesus refuses, telling the disciple to follow him and let the dead bury the dead. In both cases, it seems as if the stories had been composed in order to declare these sayings. These sayings may easily reflect actual situations in the life of Jesus, but they more certainly reflect situations and attitudes in the early Christian congregations. The former saying indicated their difficult existence in an hostile environment. The latter saying declared their determined resistance to that environment even to the point of expelling slackers. Without historical criticism, these meanings would be missed.

The disciples, fearing for their lives while on a boat in a storm, wake Jesus, who calms the storm. "And the men marveled, saying, 'What sort of man is this, that even winds and sea obey him?'" (Matthew 8: 27) Here is a combination miracle story with a preaching or missionary message. The double rebuke of Jesus, to the storm and to the disciples for their lack of faith, ends with that acclamation which a preacher can use to validate the mission of Jesus. If the storm can be seen as a metaphor for conflicts within contesting Palestinian Christian communities or between them and their compatriot Jews, the acclamation validates their faith as well as their mission, and Jesus' rebuke about lack of faith is intended to strengthen the weak. It also furnishes a great text for Christian evangelists.

Skipping the healing of two men with demons, the sixth miracle is told in a hybrid miracle-conflict form. It is the story of the paralytic cured when Jesus tells him his sins are forgiven. At that miracle, the Scribes murmur blasphemy, to which, Jesus, knowing their secret thoughts, overtly claims the power to forgive sins. The dispute over the forgiveness of serious sins roiled the early Christian communities. Some congregations absolutely denied the church could forgive sins, ever, under any circumstances, which supported the practice of delaying baptism, as Emperor Constantine did, until deathbed. This pericope is designed to show that Jesus, and, by extension, the church could forgive sins.

A simple command, "Follow me," is enough for Matthew to leave his tax booth and become a disciple. This didactic pericope displays the obvious lesson that one must surrender anything and everything to follow Jesus. The truth of the words is entirely secondary to the truth of the message.

The next pericope, Matthew 9: 10-13, is another conflict story with a pronouncement. Jesus is pictured as eating with tax collectors and sinners. When the Pharisees ask the disciples why Jesus does this, he answers them: the well do not need a physician; he came to call sinners, not the righteous. The pronouncement, "The well do not need…," defeats his enemy, the Pharisees. That this is a story composed to illustrate conflict in the life of Jesus and in the life of the Christian congregations and to settle the conflict in favor of Jesus and the Christians is unmistakably clear: there are no circumstances under which Pharisees would eat with tax collectors and sinners. The pericope should be seen as a composition (theological construct).

Another conflict-didactic narrative follows when disciples of John the Baptist asked why the disciples of Jesus did not fast. Jesus replies that they will fast once he is taken away from them. Then he claims to replace the old faith with an entirely new one when he metaphorically explains that one does not put a new patch on an old garment or put new wine into old wineskins. The followers of John the Baptist are being invited to a new life, a meaning difficult to grasp without historical criticism.

The seventh and eighth miracles may illustrate one of the few times, outside of the passion narratives, when the sequence of events is probably chronologically accurate, assuming the pericope describes an historical incident. While he was going with a ruler whose daughter had just died to his home, a woman with a discharge of blood touched the hem of Jesus' cloak hoping to be cured. Her faith saved her. At the ruler's home, Jesus dismissed the mourners and raised the girl from the dead. Two miracles in one pericope. One must marvel at the faith of the woman with the discharge of blood, how much faith she had, how it cured her. Could she represent the Christian communities under duress in Palestine? Could they be called to display similar faith? The Jesus who can raise the dead can save the congregations in distress. Is the message a simple story told in words, or is the message to keep faith in Jesus, the all powerful Son of God? Certainly, the latter message is far more important than the former, and is not attainable except through historical criticism.

The ninth and tenth miracles told of the cure of two blind men and the cure of a man unable to speak because of demonic possession.

Key Points

- The stories discussed above have little relation to one another. The connections between them are not strong. They do, however, have a purpose. Historical criticism suggests that that purpose is to illustrate the contemporary condition of Christian congregations in Palestine.
- Simple reliance on the words misses much of the message the evangelist was conveying.
- The chain of stories in Matthew could have been found in either Mark or Luke, although in a different order and with substitutions. Some authors, especially prominent form critics, suggest that the gospels were not so much composed as stitched together from pre-existing material.

- Historical criticism allows modern readers to look back into the decades before there were written gospels, an invaluable contribution.

Joachim Jeremias

Was the Last Supper a Passover Meal?

One of the several important works of this author is *The Eucharistic Words of Jesus*. On his way to determining exactly what were the eucharistic words spoken by Jesus, he must determine if the last supper was a Passover meal.

It is taken for granted that Jesus was crucified on Friday and was resurrected from the dead on Sunday. By Jewish reckoning, a day begins at sundown and ends at sundown about 24 hours later. According to Matthew, Mark and Luke, the last supper was a Passover meal eaten during the evening of Thursday, Nisan 15 (after dusk on Nissan 14 by our reckoning). According to the synoptics, Jesus was crucified during the daylight hours on Friday, Nisan 15, Passover, after eating the Passover meal on the previous evening.

The same general constraints apply to the chronology of the fourth gospel, but that gospel does not describe the last supper as a Passover meal. Therefore, the last supper would have occurred in the evening on Thursday, Nisan 14, the day before Passover. In this account, Jesus' crucifixion occurred during the daylight hours of the following day, still Nisan 14 by Jewish reckoning, the day before Passover.

To determine if the last supper was a Passover meal, Jeremias tries to narrow the range of possibilities by examining the datings of other scholars as to how many of the years between 27 and 33, the likely period when Jesus was crucified, had Nissan 14 or 15 falling on a Friday, as required by the gospel narratives. He finds the results ambiguous: the years 30 and 33 favor the Johannine chronology, and, slightly less probable, the years 31 and 30 could favor the Synoptic chronology.[55]

---

55 The year 30 appears to favor Johannine chronology and, less probably, Synoptic chronology as well. The process for establishing dates is not as straightforward as it may appear. The Jewish calendar is lunar, requiring a number of leap months.

(The years 29 and 32 must be excluded because neither Nissan 14 nor 15 fell on a Friday in those years.)

Nevertheless, Jeremias concludes that the last supper was a Passover meal and gives fourteen reasons, all based on higher criticism, why he thinks so. A few will be discussed below.

The last supper took place in Jerusalem. By way of background, at Passover, the normal population of Jerusalem, estimated to be 25,000 to 30,000, is augmented by 85,000 to 125,000 pilgrims. The city is so crowded that the meal cannot be consumed in the Temple precincts by all, and most are consumed in private homes or wherever pilgrims could squat, because the meal had to be consumed in greater Jerusalem. (The boundaries of the city were expanded at Passover to make a reasonable accommodation for the pilgrims.) Jesus did not usually stay in Jerusalem; he went to Bethany in the evenings. This time he stayed in Jerusalem, Jeremias notes, because the Passover meal must be eaten in Jerusalem.

One must appreciate the thoroughness which went into the investigation of this very first reason for designating the last supper as a Passover meal. First, using modern methods from astronomy, he determines the possibility that it could have been a Passover meal. Having found it were possible, then, using the tools of historical criticism, he builds the scenario for the meal. Applying tradition criticism to his findings thus far, he sees the behavior of Jesus as out of the ordinary, quite exceptional, and assigns a plausible reason for that exceptional behavior.

Similar Analyses

These several fold analyses occur repeatedly among Jeremias' fourteen reasons, and over and over he finds exceptional behavior linked to the exceptional circumstances of Passover. Here are a few other reasons in support of a Passover meal using similar techniques:

- eating at night—normally, two meals were taken, breakfast and the main meal in the late afternoon; but the Passover meal was always eaten at night, so this

---

The process is further complicated by the ability to actually see the first light because of atmospheric conditions.

exceptional nighttime meal is likely to be a Passover meal;

- four gospels agree that the diners reclined at table, this in an era when sitting at table was the common practice, except at Passover, and, exceptionally, other occasions;
- John 13: 10 suggests a level of ritual purity not required of ordinary meals but expected at Passover.

The Passion Narratives

Jeremias' ultimate goal is to home in on the very words Jesus spoke at the institution of the eucharist. But, as you can see from the above discussion, there are many steps along the way. To examine the passion narrative, on the way to the words of the institution of the eucharist, he starts with the general framework of the gospel according to Mark.

A reading of Mark's gospel shows a fast paced work with little coherence. If, in reading Mark we see a chronological sequence of events, it is because we have imposed that order on the document: it is not in the document itself. Concerning place, all the stories before chapter eleven seem to take place in Galilee. Jesus makes only one trip to Judea, and that is his last trip. Until late in the gospel, story after story tumbles out with loose connections between them.

When we get to chapter eleven, we have a different narrative: it is specific as to time and place; it is more or less coherently continuous, and it tells a longer story, the story of the passion, death, and resurrection of Jesus Christ. The source of the gospel has changed.

Jeremias critiques Mark's gospel in order to remove later additions to the source. The parable of the fig tree (11: 12-14) seems to interrupt the sequence of the triumphal entry into Jerusalem and the cleansing of the Temple. The discussion about the fig tree parable (11: 20-25) follows the cleansing narrative and is followed by the pericope in which the authority of Jesus is challenged. If the parable and the discussion of the parable are removed, one can read a continuous, coherent narrative. This suggests the possibility that the parable and its discussion are Markan material imposed on an earlier passion account.

Chapter twelve of Mark embodies a collection of narratives about controversy. Chapter thirteen consists of an eschatological discourse. Then, in chapter fourteen, the passion narrative resumes with the plot to kill Jesus. Jeremias describes these chapters twelve and thirteen as Markan conflations of the hypothetical primitive passion account.

Last to be dealt with are the pericopes relating to the preparation for the Passover (14: 12-16), the last supper (14: 22-25), and Gethsemane (14: 32-42). If these pericopes are misplaced, as Jeremias suspects, then there is an important finding: the passion narrative in Mark is very similar in the order of events to the passion narrative in John, leading to the conclusion of a common source.

Jeremias projects a relatively long passion narrative which begins with the triumphal entry into Jerusalem and ends with the resurrection as an ancient common source for Mark and John. This has been achieved by literary analysis of Mark's account, identifying conflations, and then comparing the more primitive account with that of John.

The anointing at Bethany occurs in John before entry into Jerusalem, but after entry in Mark. This difference in placement leads Jeremias to consider this pericope an addition to the passion narrative and not part of the ancient narrative.

In examining the texts closely, Jeremias finds a more ancient short passion narrative beginning with the arrest of Jesus. He points to the order shared so closely by Mark and John, and cites numerous summaries of the passion events which share the same order. Further, he detects later traditions in the second introduction of Judas Iscariot. In pruning these later traditions, Jeremias arrives at an ancient short passion narrative.

To sum up, higher criticism allows us to see four stages of development:

1. Kerygma (for example, I Corinthians 15: 3-5).
2. The short passion narrative beginning with the arrest of Jesus.
3. The long passion narrative beginning with the triumphal entry of Jesus.
4. Other expansions.

The Last Supper Narrative[56]

Mark's account is closely followed by Matthew, so the results of literary criticism of the former may apply to the latter. The narrative starts with the preparation mission for the Passover. Since this mission is not in the long account of the passion, it is deemed to be a later addition. On the other hand, the announcement of the traitor is in all four gospels and, therefore, part of the long account. In verses 22 to 25, Jeremias detects a radical shift in language which he interprets as very old liturgical language.

When Luke uses Mark's material, he usually follows Mark's order of events, unlike Matthew, . In examining the account of the last supper, Jeremias detects four differences in the order of events. To have so many differences (when differences in order are unusual) in so short a space leads Jeremias to conclude that from verse 14 on, Luke followed a different passion story. Furthermore, he sees two different sources for verses 15-18 and 19-20, the former from Luke's Palestinian source, and the latter from the liturgy. The sayings section (verses 24-38) which follows almost to the end of the chapter comprises two sources as shown by the change from the earlier "Simon" to the later "Peter."

Chapter thirteen of John's gospel consists of two parts, the foot washing and its two interpretations (verses 1-5, 6-11, and 12 to 20), and the announcement of betrayal. The betrayal announcement is part of the long passion narrative and, therefore, ancient. However, the two interpretations of the foot washing indicate this pericope underwent development and is, therefore, later.

These are the fruits of higher criticism of the narrative of the last supper.

1. Mark 14: 22-24, commonly thought of as the words of institution, are the earliest parts of the last supper story, possibly as old as the kerygma itself.
2. Mark 14: 17-21, the announcement of the coming betrayal of Jesus, is in all four gospels and should be seen as a part of the long account of the passion.
3. Everything else is likely to be:

---

56   Mark 14: 12-26; Matthew 26: 17-30; Luke 22: 7-39; John 13: 1-30.

a. Part of an early particular tradition, such as the washing of the feet,

b. Part composition, such as the table conversation in Luke, or

c. Part conflation or expansion, such as the mission to prepare for the Passover.

Raymond E. Brown, SS

It is not hard to see how Raymond Brown's theory on the development of the *Gospel according to John* relies on some of the techniques of higher criticism. We do not pretend to know how Brown arrived at his theory, but, considering the order in which he presented his theory in his <u>Introduction</u> to *The Gospel according to John I – XII,*[57] redaction criticism could have been a starting point. Historical and literary criticism lead to the bulk of the remainder of the theory. Nonetheless, a relevant part of the key points of that discussion is provided below.

*   An original, authentic, Palestinian tradition, possibly beginning with the Apostle John.
*   Development over time through teaching and preaching into narratives.
*   The anonymous evangelist developed the first edition of the gospel, possibly as early as 75 – 85.
*   The evangelist redacted his first edition to account for current issues and problems, especially the expulsion of Jewish Christians from the synagogues.
*   Finally, a disciple of the evangelist added ancient material, lest it be lost, to produce the final gospel, 90-110.

Rudolf Bultmann

Everything which has be said before in some way prepares for what follows. Rudolf Bultmann departs from the methods of expression of Jeremias and Brown. The latter would be considered "orthodox" or

---

57 Previously cited.

"more orthodox" than the former, but that description is not useful. One must look at Bultmann (and Dibelius and others) on his own ground. Our presuppositions are of no importance to devoted theologians like Bultmann or to scripture scholars like Brown or Jeremias, learned contemporaries of Bultmann. Bultmann presents himself as a believing Christian, but the way he expresses his belief is thoroughly contemporary, or at least, mid- twentieth century. [58]

The typical way we try to understand the bible is to read it in translation with the faith we bring to it. An example of what we might see is that the miracles of Jesus authenticate his mission. Or, we may conclude from our reading that we are a part of the Kingdom of God, that vast spiritual network of believing Christians who work to promote God's work on earth.

Our reading would, in Bultmann's view, miss the underlying truths of the message because we relied on the words rather than the message of the distant writer.

Bultmann, a believing Christian, proposes, and is known for his commitment, to demythologize the gospels. The notion that mythology is incorporated into the New Testament may shock believing Christians, but Bultmann is very serious in his charge.

He is confronted, like the second, third and fourth generations of Christians, by the fact that Jesus has not returned, there has been no Rapture, and life, allowing for expected slow development over two thousand years, is pretty much the same as it always has been, "solitary, poor, nasty, brutish, and short," in the words of Thomas Hobbes.

One of his conclusions is that the apocalyptic expectations in the New Testament are a myth. History has proved them wrong. We are here.

The Kingdom of God in the New Testament is a myth. The brutality of nation to nation, religion to religion, person to person, and the clueless proclamations, prognostications and personal moral hypocrisy of highly regarded Christian and other leaders are facts of life. History has demolished the Kingdom of God.

---

58   It would be a serious injustice to Bultmann to dismiss his views on the basis of the very abbreviated account here. Rudolf Bultmann was a person of immense learning and great subtlety, and it is appropriate to engage him directly through one or more of his writings. You might be persuaded, or not, but your knowledge will expand.

The virgin birth and the incarnation of a pre-existent God are both myths. They are totally outside of everything we know about the world and the natural order of things.

The notion of a deity who intervenes in human affairs is a myth, for the same reason: we know how the world works, and there is no reason to believe in frequent or repeated interventions of the deity in the affairs of men or in the rotation of planets around the sun. While we are here, let's dismiss entirely the notion of miracles for the same reason. Again, while we are at it, let's dismiss the idea that a deity created the world. Science provides a more plausible explanation.

The idea of Satan and his army of devils corrupting the human race is a myth. We know there are plenty of reasons why people do the terrible things they do to one another. How many have been slaughtered in the name of God? Satan is not needed.

We can now see our planet from space. Heaven is not the top storey of a three level condominium, hell being the bottom. Fact: there are not four columns holding up the vault of the heavens, as was commonly believed by the ancients, including the authors of our sacred scriptures.

What about the raising of Lazarus or the widow's son? Myths.

What about Jesus, his resurrection and the empty tomb? Have you, or any credible witness, ever seen a person rise from the dead? The empty tomb stories are apologetic myths.

Bultmann maintains that when we accept the myths of a past age as defining our hermeneutics (the rules and methods by which we analyze scriptures), we cannot understand the real and true message of scripture. The writers of those times were writing what they knew in the world which they knew. There were many miracle workers then. The sun revolved around the earth then. There were a number of literary references to several god-men then. The redactors of the gospels could not imagine quantum mechanics or a big bang then—nor could we until about a century ago.

The core of Bultmann's critique is hermeneutics. We cannot understand the true message of the New Testament if we insist upon clinging to the myths and the world views of the authors and redactors of the New Testament.

What then? Are we to dismiss the New Testament? That is not

Bultmann's choice. He believes there is a valid message for the world, but it will never be understood if we cling to the myths which surround it.

It is far easier to explain demythologizing the scriptures than to explain Bultmann's belief system. That depends on the eschatological now. This is the moment when each individual faces the fact of Jesus Christ, not in the good news of the gospels, but in his own individual existence. Look through the epistles of Paul and even through the Gospel of John. In the former, there is almost no contact with the historical Jesus. In the latter, the contact is overwhelmed by the repeated poetic declarations of salvation now, at this moment, for those who believe.

The past is unimportant, and to hope in the future is to turn away from Jesus now and to be condemned. One cannot rely on oneself. The eschatological now demands that the person acknowledge the fact of Jesus and rely completely upon the grace of God which surely flows from this recognition. The person is not persuaded to faith: that would be condemnation. The rationalization inherent in persuasion convicts the person of lack of faith. Faith is a gift resulting from kerygma, but all within the individual at a given *now*. The person must rely completely in faith: there is no next; there is only now. Here we find a faith equal to Tertullian's when he said that we must believe in the resurrection of Jesus because it is impossible.

Bultmann makes much about the hiddenness of the salvific process. How could it be anything else? It involves the individual's understanding of oneself, admitting the need for repentance, and casting oneself without reservation upon the mercy of God through faith in Jesus Christ.

Bultmann believes that this process leads to a life of service in Christ.

Key Points

- In order to understand the message of scripture, it is necessary to demythologize scripture, that is, to cast off the language and understandings of the pre-scientific world which produced the scripture.

- Once past thinking about myths, the true meaning of scripture becomes evident: Christ, sent by God for our salvation, confronts us to rely completely on him in faith. He says this over and over.
- This process is entirely individual, interior, and unseen by anyone. It occurs in the eschatological now when the need for repentance is recognized and the grace of God bestows faith.

Chapter Eight: From Congregation to Church

In the Beginning

What was it like in the days after the crucifixion of Jesus? Paul, writing in the fifties and sixties doesn't tell us, and the gospels which we know were not yet written. These gospels, along with others used by the early churches, and the *Acts of the Apostles*, along with other attempts at historical reconstruction popular in the second and third centuries, attempt to fill in what happened, but scholars have reasons to question that these accounts are historically accurate. When considering the emergence of the church from the chaos of the crucifixion, the best sources we have are the letters of Paul, the gospels, and some other documents which were at one time considered scripture by various churches and church leaders in the second, third, and fourth centuries.

The Teaching of the Lord to the Gentiles by the Twelve Apostles is described as "a church manual of primitive Christianity or of some section of it."[59] The title itself gives some idea of the dilemmas scholars face in developing the "original" text of an ancient document. The *Teaching* itself is very old, as we shall see below, but the text is based on one complete text in Greek and a fragment of a Latin translation. The Greek text dates to the mid-eleventh century. The first line of the text speaks of the teaching of the twelve apostles. However, the *Teaching* is cited by several ancient authors as *The Teaching of the Apostles*, omitting the Twelve. The editors adopted the earlier citations as opposed to the text because age—nearness to the

---

59   53 *The Apostolic Fathers*, previously cited, p. 215.

time described—is one of the most important criteria in selecting which reading of a text should be preferred.

The editors believe the *Teaching* dates to the end of the first century or the first quarter of the second century because of the language and subject matter. Part of the *Teaching* gives rules or advice for hospitality to itinerant prophets and preachers. The good news was preached, usually in synagogues, by itinerant prophets and preachers. Prophets and preachers would go from village to village and preach in the local synagogue or private home, or both, whichever characterized the practice of the local congregation. These were welcome to stay a day or two, but if they stayed three days or asked for money, they were false prophets. Such advice suggests the absence of permanent local clergy.

The *Teaching* uses the Greek word "episcopos," which literally means "overseer" and later came to mean "bishop," as a synonym for "presbuteros," which is commonly translated "elder" and later understood to be a priest. Thus, the *Teaching* couples bishops with priests and deacons (as does Paul at times), leading to the conclusion that these offices had not yet been developed to the point that they were different from one another. When discussing the eucharistic thanksgiving, the *Teaching* suggests that a meal followed, which was characteristic of some very early congregations. The *Teaching* is thought to have been composed in Syria or Palestine.

As of the time of the *Teaching*, church offices had not developed except, perhaps, for a class of servers broadly called deacons. Recall Paul's description of his visit to Jerusalem. He went to speak to men of influence. He called James, Peter and John pillars. Pillars may hold up a roof, but they do not govern a congregation in the same way as a monarchical bishop. That office had yet to be established in Paul's time and, apparently, in the place where the *Teaching* was written or compiled, at the time when it was written or compiled.

In another place at around the same time when the *Teaching* was written or compiled, we get a different picture of the emergence of churches from congregations.

"The Apostles received the gospel for us from the Lord Jesus Christ; Jesus Christ was sent forth from God. So then Christ is from God, and the Apostles are from Christ. Both therefore came of the will of God in the appointed order. Having therefore received a charge, and having been fully assured through the resurrection of our Lord Jesus Christ and confirmed in the word of God with full assurance of the Holy Ghost, they went forth with the glad tidings that the kingdom of God should come. So preaching everywhere in country and town, they appointed their first fruits, when they had proved them by the Spirit, to be bishops and deacons unto them that should believe. And they did this in no new fashion; for indeed it had been written concerning bishops and deacons from very ancient times; for thus saith the scripture in a certain place, *I will appoint their bishops in righteousness and their deacons in faith.*" [60]

This excerpt is from an epistle sent by the Church at Rome to the Church at Corinth. It is ascribed to Clement I, who is counted among the early bishops of Rome. Many scholars think it dates from the year 96. It was accepted as scripture by a number of congregations and is included in one of the earliest surviving codices of the New Testament. The excerpt has a number of important points characteristic of proto-catholic Christianity.

1. The apostles received a gospel from Jesus.
2. Jesus was commissioned by God.
3. The received gospel was validated by the resurrection of Jesus and the testimony (?) of the Holy Ghost.
4. The apostles went forth to preach to the world.
5. When the apostles left a mission place, they appointed bishops and deacons to minister to the congregation.
6. Bishops and deacons were appointed from very ancient times.

The argument is easy to follow. The good news came from God through Christ to his apostles who passed it on to their authorized successors. Clement does not give a reference to the "scripture" he cites. We will examine the elements in more detail later, but one can easily see how different a picture of early Christianity Clement paints from that of the *Teaching*.

How do we reconcile the two different pictures?

---

60 *Apostolic Fathers*, Epistle of Clement, p. 75.

Why should they be reconciled? For theological reasons? There were multiple pictures, many different congregations with many different ideas about the nature of Christ, his relationship with God, and the governance of congregations, just as there are today. In chapter four we mentioned a number of Gnostic Christian congregations. These are by no means all the shades of Gnostic Christian teaching. These congregations all believed that they had the authority of Jesus Christ and God for their teachings.

Also in that chapter, we spoke of Palestinian Christians as if they were different from Greek speaking Christians. They were different. In the earliest times, there were no monarchical bishops. There were no monarchical bishops in the contemporary Greek speaking congregations, but they evolved. The only Palestinian congregations which apparently survived expulsion from the synagogues used gospels not accepted as canonical by the catholic church. These did not clearly develop the office of monarchical bishop. Inasmuch as these congregations observed Jewish law to apparently widely varying degrees, it is likely that the leadership style characteristic of the synagogue perdured. There is no evidence that these congregations were influenced by the Roman church or any Greek speaking church. These congregations all believed that they had the authority of Jesus Christ and God for their teachings.

Observance of Jewish law would have proposed profound theological problems for the proto-catholic congregations. Even to suggest that the Law offered a gateway to salvation contradicted the core of the developing proto-catholic theology. To the extent that these congregations survived long enough to be excommunicated from the holy, Roman Catholic Church, they were shunned by proto-catholic churches.

We must recall that Palestine nourished Gnostic Christian congregations and, possibly, some proto-catholic congregations as well as the particularly Palestinian Christian congregations with their attachments to Jewish law. Palestine hosted a veritable smorgasbord of Christianities. These congregations all believed that they had the authority of Jesus Christ and God for their teachings.

It is useful to recall that Palestine was the homeland of Jesus, his family, and the Apostles, and their families. While there are many legends portraying the Apostles as great travelers and missionaries, one has to believe that their first mission lay to the Jews, the chosen people of Yahweh, of whom they were. Perhaps, as Palestinian Christians were expelled from the synagogues, occurring gradually around the years 80 to 90, the Apostles perforce travelled, but by then, it is probable that most, if not all of them were dead. Isn't it difficult to conceive of the development of so many kinds of Christianity in Palestine without the guidance or at least tolerance of some of the Apostles? They all associated with Jesus. They all heard the same message. Three times Peter denied that he knew Jesus. If Thomas had to see the wounds of the risen Jesus and if Judas Iscariot sold out his teacher, why not Bartholomew, Philip, or James, or.... Doesn't it strain credulity to suppose otherwise? These congregations all believed that they had the authority of Jesus Christ and God for their teachings.

Key Points

- The origins of Christianity lie in Palestine.
- The good news was preached by Apostles, prophets and preachers.
- There is no very early evidence of monarchical bishops, priests, or even deacons as the diaconate is conceived as an ecclesiastical office.
- There is evidence that some places had no resident preachers.
- Palestinian congregations included Gnostic Christians as well as more or less Torah-observant Christians. Some assume that there were proto-catholic congregations as well.
- All of these congregations believed that they had the authority of Jesus Christ and God for their teachings.
- The role of the Apostles in the Palestinian congregations is obscure and problematic.
- There is no evidence of extended[61] proto-catholic theology or ecclesiastical organization in the epistles of Paul, the four canonical gospels, or the *Teaching of the Apostles*.

---

61 By "extended" we mean to include for consideration the several arguable

- The development of proto-catholic congregations began late in the first century, by which time early Christians in Palestine had been expelled from the synagogues. This suggests the possibility that there were no proto-catholic congregations in Palestine.
- The *First Epistle of Clement* (96 CE) constitutes the first written evidence of proto-catholic organization. Even at this point in time, there is no evidence of extended proto-catholic theology.

The War on Gnosticism

Nor is it permissible to suppose that outside of Palestine everything was neat and clean. It wasn't. Orthodox congregations of second, third and fourth generation Christians generally lacked the language, the philosophical underpinnings to support speculative theology. Gnosticism, on the other hand, was some five hundred years old when it encountered the Christ event. Gnostics developed Christologies very quickly because their philosophy furnished them the conceptual tools.

Part of the earliest problem proto-catholics had with Roman authorities was their apocalypticism. Since this world was passing away, Christians regarded sexual and social relations as relatively unimportant, and the accumulation of wealth or knowledge appeared to be suspiciously ambitious and vain. In addition to their apocalypticism, another problem lay in their exclusivism and sense of chosenness which the Christians took from their mother religion. These attitudes tended to alienate both pagans and Jews.

However, proto-catholics had one enormous advantage over Gnostics: there was a flourishing proto-catholic congregation in Rome, the seat of the Empire. In an era of primitive communications and ignorance

---

propositions regarding Jesus' messianic consciousness or the even more controversial propositions regarding his disciples' understanding of him. Extended theology would embrace such issues as sacraments, especially the nature of sacraments, the understanding of God's grace, the person of Jesus as man, god, or god-man, the trinity, and similar controversies.

of any systematic theology, the Empire's understanding of Christianity would be deeply colored, if not determined, by its observations of and communications with the Roman church. It is perfectly plausible to see that the Roman congregation was among the first to develop a more or less monarchical bishopric, copying the kind of government organization it saw in front of itself, in order to communicate with the Empire. It was a matter of survival at first, growing into a matter of self-promotion as army commanders fought each other to become Emperor, developing into religious dominance in the fourth century Empire as the handmaiden of the Emperor, and, with the passing of the Empire, culminating into both a civil and religious government. This same "convenience factor" is how the proto-catholic Roman church came to dominate, more or less, the theology of the Empire, which usually cared little or nothing about theology.

Proto-catholics waged unrelenting war on Gnostics for several reasons.

- They could not admit the possibility that people continued to have a direct connection to the deity valid for the community of believers. They had to insist that the period of revelation had closed. Why?
- They insisted that only they, the proto-catholic bishops, knew the true gospel transmitted by Jesus to his Apostles and their successors, this in an age when not all gospels had been written, when not all gospels had been widely disseminated, when not all proto-catholic bishops shared a commonly agreed upon canon of scripture, and when not all proto-catholic bishops shared a commonly agreed upon creed.
- Their apology for Christianity saw it as a fulfillment of Hebrew Bible prophesies. Gnostics generally disregarded the Hebrew Bible as the product of the evil god Yahweh.

Some Apologies

Among the earliest Gnostic theologies, Docetism embraced two separate theologies. Fundamentally, both taught that God could not die. In one form, the person of Jesus was the first aeon of God, and the material body of Jesus was a phantasm, an illusion. The second form, preached by Cerinthus, Valentinus, and others in slightly different forms held that Jesus was human and Christ was divine, that Christ invested Jesus at his baptism and perforce abandoned Jesus on the cross, for God cannot die.

This alarming development—Gnostic theology—caused the orthodox congregations to adopt defensive strategies which produced the great apologists of orthodoxy. These apologies became the first fruits of orthodox theological speculation.

Ignatius of Antioch (ob. 107?) is one of the most important proto-catholics because of the seven letters he wrote while on his way to execution in Rome. Ignatius fiercely defends the developing episcopal organization of the churches and repeatedly urges respect and support for the bishops. He thinks it important that there be only one bishop in a community, leading, eventually, to the separation of the offices of bishop and priest. The exact nature of the episcopacy he advocated is obscure, although he compares the bishop to God the Father when urging submission of the congregation to the bishop. The bishop cannot be monarchical if obedience is voluntary, nor does it appear to have been an appointive office. He postulates a council of presbyters who act in place of the Apostles, and who probably elect the bishop, if the franchise were not even more popular. He counts himself among the deacons. His advocacy of pastors is rooted in his desire to crush Docetism.

His consistent advocacy of respect for bishops, with the notable exception of his epistle to the Romans, can be seen as evidence of the development of the office of bishop in the early second century. A form of the office probably had developed in Rome around the turn of the first century, and was championed by Rome as the ideal form of church government among proto-catholic congregations. Ignatius' pleas for respect for the (new?) office can be seen as part of this effort to promote the developing office of bishop.

Justin Martyr (100?-166?) defended Christianity against the pagans in a twofold argument, first claiming innocence of the crimes alleged, and second, remediating the ignorance of the Romans of the ethical superiority of Christianity. The *First Apology*, directed to the Emperor and his chosen successors, is directed against the charges that Christians are atheists (that is, they do not participate in the worship of the state's gods) and are indifferent to the welfare of the state. The *Second Apology* covers similar ground: Romans do not know, and therefore do not appreciate the moral excellence of the Christians. Another work, his *Dialogue with Trypho* attempts to convince his Jewish adversary of the truth of the Christian religion.

Athenagoras, writing about the year 177, refutes the similar charges, atheism, immorality and cannibalism (connected with a misunderstanding of the eucharist) by pointing out that Christians worship a truly spiritual God, not gods made by men or mere men deified by men, and that they avoid even the thought of evil as much as evil itself.

Irenaeus (140?-203?) refuted the Gnostics Marcion and Valentinus in part by claiming that there had been many bishops in many places since the time of the Apostles, and that not one of them was a Gnostic. He claimed that none of the Gnostics believed that the Word had become flesh, which would be true since Gnostics abhorred flesh and all things material. Irenaeus quotes a number of phrases found in a variety of New Testament writings and insists upon four and only four gospels. Irenaeus was arguing for the adoption of an orthodox canon to counter Marcion's canon.

Clement of Alexandria (150-211) headed the very influential catechetical school in Alexandria. His works include a presentation of the gospel to educated Greeks, a catechism, and a spiritual guide for mature believers.

His successor, Origin (185-254), established himself as the most advanced theologian and biblical scholar of the third century by the volume of his works and their quality. Origin is regarded by many as the first great catholic theologian. He developed the methods of exegesis initiated by his predecessor into a theory of allegorical interpretation: a text has meaning on three levels, the literal, the ethical, and the spiritual. His writings include: *Hexapla* (harmony of six versions of the Hebrew Bible), *Miscellanies*, and *On the Resurrection*. He worked diligently against the Gnostic Valentinus. *Contra Celsum* (248?) vindicates Christianity against pagan attack. His most original work, *On First Principles*, is the one which caused him to be suspected of heresy by later theologians, even though he described this work as speculative and designed only for well educated and strong Christians. Origin suggested the pre-existence of souls, but did not teach the transmigration of souls, or the incorporation of rational souls in animal bodies. He taught that redemption is an educational process, and a grand education by God is possible even to Satan, who retains free will. Redemption restores fallen souls from matter to spirit, from image to reality. On free will, neither heaven nor hell can be absolute because Christ's work remains unfinished until he has subdued all to himself. Then, the whole drama may begin again. It seems that Origin helped to invent some of our concepts on the Trinity, but the person of the Son was probably subordinate to the person of the Father in his thinking.

Key Points

- By way of background, the Gnostic theologies differed from one another in some important respects. We see these differences because Gnostics, having a philosophical language, were able to express their theologies more precisely than proto-catholics.
- By way of background, Gnostics rather uniformly believed that few persons could gain the requisite secret knowledge which would save them. Also, most Gnostic sects were rigorously ascetic, diminishing their appeal to ordinary people. These two features combined to give Gnosticism a decidedly elitist posture. The nature of their self-righteousness hindered communication among Gnostic congregations: each one thought it was superior to the others.
- The proto-catholic apologists, on the other hand, offered general defenses against persecution. There were

discussions of baptism and the eucharist, but these were, again, general defenses and not elaborated discussions of how these sacraments came into being or how they worked in the contemporary world. Nevertheless, these and similar apologies constitute the rude beginnings of proto-catholic theology.

- Unlike Gnostics, proto-catholics, as their name suggests, were out to save the whole world. In pursuit of their mission, they communicated often with one another, mostly, at times, about how to combat Gnosticism. Lacking means and opportunity in the face of Gnostic sects, they did not contend among themselves (very much) about the subtleties of their beliefs, especially inasmuch as their beliefs had not been elaborated dialectically. (There was a famous controversy about the dating of Easter, but that was a matter of discipline rather than faith.)

- An hypothesis: if it is correct to say that the philosophical preparedness of the Gnostics resulted in vigorous debates about the nuances of Gnostic theology, then it is possible to suggest that as proto-catholic theology developed, differences among proto-catholic congregations would become as common and as extreme as the differences among the Gnostic congregations. See below.

Who is This Person Jesus Christ?

"Is not this the carpenter's son? Is not his mother called Mary? And are not his brothers James and Joseph and Simon and Judas? And are not his sisters with us? Where did this man get all these things?" (Matthew 13: 55-56)

"In the beginning was the Word, and the Word was with God, and the Word was God. He was in the beginning with God. All things were made through him, and without him was not anything made that was made." (John: 1: 1-3)

127

"In those days Jesus came from Nazareth of Galilee and was baptized by John in the Jordan. And when he came up out of the water, immediately he saw the heavens being torn open and the Spirit descending on him like a dove. And a voice came from heaven, 'You are my beloved Son; with you I am well pleased.'" (Mark: 1: 9-11)

"And at the ninth hour Jesus cried with a loud voice, 'Eloi, Eloi, lema sabachthani?' which means, 'My God, my God, why have you forsaken me?'" (Mark 15:34)

One could go on to elaborate other expressions of the person of Jesus in the gospels, but these are enough for our consideration here. The first expression is the natural and ordinary reaction of common folk trying to comprehend a miracle worker whom they had known previously as an ordinary young man. They knew his family. What was so special about him? Is he not an ordinary human being? Their incredulity is evidence of his ordinariness.

The second suggests that the Word existed from all eternity as God. The placement of this hymn or poem seems to identify the pre-existent Word with Jesus as the incarnation of the Word, as the incarnation of the pre-existent God.

The third testimony suggests the possibility that Jesus is the Son of God adopted at his baptism, not a pre-existent God. Alternative texts are more clearly Adoptionist.

The fourth was often cited by Gnostics to show how Christ, the spirit, separated from Jesus, the material, at crucifixion. John's hymn on the Word was also given a Gnostic interpretation, the pre-existent Word being identified as the first emanation of God, not God himself, pure spirit.

Four testimonies. Five possibilities. It is granted that a person of a particular faith could interpret these four and other gospel citations as proof of the divinity of Jesus. It is granted that a skeptic could interpret these four and other gospel citations as proof of the humanity of Jesus. Exegesis follows hermeneutics, that is, the explanation of a particular passage is driven by the rules for explaining that passage.

The proto-catholic church, by the fourth century, developed the theory of the hypostatic union, namely, that the person of Jesus embraced both godhead and humanity. Inasmuch as *hypostasis*, the root of hypostatic, means personality when speaking of a person, or substance/ nature/essence when not speaking of a person, two persons in one person is indeed a mystery. A mystery is a proposition which defies human logic, and a religious truth known only by divine revelation. This issue is debated today, but in the fourth century of Christianity, debate often took the form of armed compulsion, to the point of exile or martyrdom.

Key Points

- Exegesis, the interpretation of a text, depends upon hermeneutics, the rules governing exegesis. Multiple interpretations of a text are available to a range of hermeneutics. See Afterword for a few examples.
- Theological exploration of the person of Jesus Christ led the catholic churches to the conclusion that two persons, God and man, are present in one person, Jesus Christ. This is indeed a mystery, a proposition which defies human logic and a religious truth known only by divine revelation.

Competing Orthodoxies

Second Repentance[62]

The Decian persecution (251) raised a thorny issue for proto-catholic churches. Many Christians avoided the persecution by hiding their Christianity—a mortal sin according to the orthodox—or, as if it could possibly be worse—conformed to the persecutor's requirements, sacrificing to idols, worshipping the Emperor, eating meat sacrificed to idols, and so forth. Apparently, many congregations believed that they could not forgive sin in the case of a second repentance. This rigorous attitude helps to explain in part the origins of the cult of martyrdom. In part, this attitude was based on Hebrews 6: 4-6: "For it is impossible,

---

62 First repentance acknowledges a sinful past life and leads to baptism and membership in the church.

in the case of those who have once been enlightened, who have tasted the heavenly gift, and have shared in the Holy Spirit, and have tasted the goodness of the word of God and the powers of the age to come, and have fallen away, to restore them again to repentance, since they are crucifying once again the Son of God to their own harm and holding him up to contempt."[63]

There had been, however, a growing relaxation in church discipline among the many churches. Many lapsed catholics, when the persecution ended, wanted to return to their churches. With the election of Pope Cornelius, a person who favored forgiveness of sin, Novatian, a rigorous priest, secured his election to the papacy, creating the first known anti-pope. Novatian insisted that churches did not have the power to forgive sin.

Tertullian, the brilliant Latin apologist, had left the catholic church over this very issue. He insisted that the church had no power to forgive such sins as sacrificing to the Emperor, eating meat sacrificed to idols, adultery, and similar sexual behaviors. By the time of Decius (shortly after Tertullian), some churches had come to believe this rigor was incorrect. This theological development may have affected the wording of the gospels (chapter five). (Recall, there was no New Testament canon widely accepted by the proto-catholic church. While the gospels of Matthew, Mark, Luke, and John, were highly regarded at this time and often elevated to the level of scripture, their texts were not exact, and other gospels were similarly regarded.) Valerian (259-260) also instituted a persecution, bringing a new urgency to the issue in a relatively short period of time.

One authority estimates that at the end of the Valerian persecution Christians comprised 8% to 9% of the population, but were concentrated in urban areas.[64] This concentration in urban areas tended to bring attention to Christians and their behaviors. Martyrdom may have provided entertainment for the populace, but, on the whole at his point in time, it did not promote the peace and stability desired by the ruling authorities. These days, any powerful army commander could be a threat to the Emperor.

---

63   This Epistle, formerly ascribed to Paul, and now recognized as a form other than that of an epistle, may have been composed as late as the final decade of the first century, and, therefore, of no matter to the persecutions under Nero (54-68) and Domition (81-96).

64   *Greek and Roman Civilization*. Encyclopedia Britannica (15th edition, 1995), vol. 20, p. 330.

The persecution ordered by Diocletion (284-305), the last and the most virulent, resulted in the deaths of perhaps 3,500 Christians, and the torture and imprisonment of many more.[65] Again, second repentance became a major issue as many Christians had lapsed and wished to be reunited to their churches. Like other persecutions, this one was enforced with widely varying degrees of enthusiasm. Although the persecution principally affected the eastern churches, the churches in North Africa, that is, the Latin churches, stridently opposed forgiveness for second repentance. They, too, had been affected by the persecution and had, in the past, tended toward asceticism and rigor.

A certain Caecilian, an apostate Christian who had re-entered the church in Carthage, was elected bishop there, to the outrage of the rigorists in that community and much of northern Africa. The latter group elected its own bishop, Majorinus, succeeded shortly by Donatus, by whose name Donatists are known. Donatists held that sacraments administered by lapsed Christians had no validity. Many cities elected two bishops, one Donatist, the other catholic (as the party would come to be known). The schism lasted into the sixth century.

Key Point

- There was a time when many proto-catholic congregations believed their congregations, relying in part upon Hebrews 6: 4-6, could not forgive sin. They conceived Christianity as a call to repentance where past sin was forgiven by baptism, and the grace (an undefined term at that time) of baptism conferred strength until the parousia.

Person or Essence

Although the concept of hypostasis/personality/substance became a huge issue in the fourth century, Sabellius introduced that notion early in the third century. Sabelius taught that God is one. He believed that we know God in his aspects as Father (creator), Son (redeemer), and

---

65 Frend, W. H. C. *Martyrdom and Persecution* as reported in *Wikipedia*, "Diocletianic Persecution."

Holy Spirit (sanctifier), but God is one. These aspects of God constituted his personae, his masks, but God is one. He was content with the unscriptural word consubstantial (*homoousios* in Greek), meaning "of the same substance" because he believed in the unity of God. His teaching is often referred to as *patripassionism,* a derogatory term which means that God the Father suffered death on the cross. This constituted the charge against Sabellius.

Arius, a fourth century cleric, also taught that God is one. Since Christ was begotten by the Father, Arius saw the Father as anterior in time to the Son. The Son is, therefore, the first being in creation, the only begotten, and the creator of all other beings. (Notice the similarity to Gnostic thinking.) Emperor Constantine, who seemed to lean toward Arianism, convoked the Council of Nicea (325) and ordered it to settle the dispute because the dispute was creating ferment in the Empire. Arianism had captured the minds of masses of ordinary people because they could understand it. Competing churches had been established in Egypt and beyond.

That the Emperor was interested in peace and security rather than theology may be evidenced by his burning, completely unread by him, before the Council a large number of complaints (petitions) by bishops and clerics of both Arian and Catholic persuasion appealing to him to rule in their favor. Following this dramatic act, he ordered the Council to settle the matter. The Council produced the Nicene Creed. The fact that the creed favored the Catholic party rather than the Emperor's preferred Arian party is further evidence of the Emperor's concern for peace and stability over theology. Since Constantine convened and presided over the Council of Nicea, to which the western churches sent only eight representatives, two of whom were presbyters representing the Roman church, Constantine's priority for peace and tranquility clearly triumphed over his preference for Arianism. Another way of stating these results is that the Nicene Creed is a political compromise, but not a theological, compromise. (Theologians, as a rule, do not compromise.)

The Nicene Creed, which was edited and enlarged by future Councils, adopted the consubstantial (*homoousios*) formula, in spite of the fact that it had been used by Sabellius a century earlier. This was the same Sabellius whom the proto-catholic churches condemned for using the term, "consubstantial" to mean the same thing as it meant to the Niceans. Sabellius used the term to signify the unity of God. The Nicean Council used it to a similar purpose, to signify that the Father and the Son have the same essence. The Niceans, however, allowed two meanings, person as well as essence, as if they were different. This is theology, the application of philosophical principles to the study of a purely spiritual, unbounded God, unknowable without his self-revelation.

The Nicean Council with its creed seemed to Constantine to have solved the dispute. He gave up his personal feeling for Arius, whom he could understand, and accepted the Nicean formula, which lay outside human reason, for the prize of peace and tranquility. Nicea should have led to the peace and tranquility he so ardently wished. In fact, the dispute continued, even up to the present day, and certainly to the end of the fourth century when his son, Constantius, secured a decree proclaiming Arianism from the Council of Constantinople (360).

Appolinaris (ob. 390), a noted opponent of Arianism, believed that the divine nature overwhelmed the human soul of Jesus. He did not believe that a rational human soul would have a purpose or could function in the divine Jesus. He could not admit two natures, distinct but not separate, combined in one person, the Nicene formula. In emphasizing the divinity of Jesus and the unity of his person, Appolinaris taught that Jesus Christ's actions reflected only the godhead.

Key Points

- As theological reflection developed among proto-catholic congregations, the person of Jesus came to be seen as divine, not the first born of creation, not the adopted Son of God, but the actual Son of God, begotten by the Father, sharing the essence of the Father, and that, from all eternity, without temporal difference from the Father.

- At the same time, the person of Jesus fully embraced the personality or essence of humankind. He did not appear to be human: he was completely human. If, contrary to Jewish culture, Jesus never married, he surely experienced the perturbations of adolescent and adult males.

- This theology required the hypostatic (essence, nature, person) union of the divine essence and the human personality in one person. It cannot be explained: two persons in one person or two essences in one essence is indeed a mystery.
- Affirming the pre-existent divinity of Jesus the Christ presented another issue, namely, how to preserve the unity of God. If God the Father is the creator of the visible universe, and God the Son is the Redeemer of that universe, then the only way to escape the conclusion that there are two gods is to affirm a mystery, a proposition which defies human logic, and so forth. In this case, three persons (adding the Holy Spirit) share one divine person or essence, arriving at the satisfying number three and avoiding any hint of warring dualisms (good v. evil, light v. darkness, flesh v. spirit, and so forth).

Other Controversies

Concupiscence and sexual immorality have hypnotized Christians from our very beginning. The apocalypticism of the first believers resulted in Paul's harangue in I Corinthians 7: 26-31, and a number of other passages in which he inveighs against sexuality. The Gnostic sects, hating matter and valuing spirit, were largely ascetic in their practices, some forbidding even marriage. Many proto-catholics felt the same way, including Tertullian, a brilliant apologist who left his proto-catholic congregation because he saw it as morally soft.

Pelagius, a British monk living in Rome in the first decade of the 5th century, denied the theory of original sin, namely, that death and concupiscence resulted from Adam's fall. He taught that man was able to avoid sin and attain salvation on his own, and that the Law is equal to the gospel as a path to heaven. He, however, was not equal to his primary opponent, Augustine of Hippo (a reformed sexaholic?) who utterly crushed him with the Pauline pronouncements of unmerited salvation, the free grace of God, and predestination.

Nestorius, Bishop of Constantinople, in 428/429 objected to Mary's title as "Mother of God." He taught that Mary was the mother of Jesus the Christ, but not the mother of God. The controversy is a throwback to the confusion about the person of Jesus: Nestorius considered himself a Catholic and agreed with the condemnation by Catholics that God did not die on the cross. But, if God did not die on the cross, then God was not born of Mary. God existed from all eternity; Mary did not. Nestorius held that in the person of Jesus dwelled two distinct persons or natures, God and man. Nestorianism captured much of the eastern church and was defeated only by the spread of Islam. Nestorians survive today, like most of the Christianities described here, usually in smaller, isolated groups.

There were two related attempts in the fifth and sixth centuries to avoid the mystery of the hypostatic union of two natures in one person. Eutyches, the archimandrite (abbot or overseer, equivalent in rank to a bishop) of a monastery in Constantinople and known for combating Nestorius, came to deny, around 450, that Jesus had both a human nature and a divine nature. Eutyches taught that the two natures in Christ became fused into one nature, the divine. This theory is called Eutychianism, after Eutyches, or monophysitism, which means one nature.

Monothelitism is the belief that one will, the divine will, energized Jesus, that the person of Jesus conducted himself through the operation of his divine will only, that he lacked an operative human voluntary faculty. This position was put forward as a possible compromise between catholic orthodoxy as declared by a succession of church councils, especially Chalcedon, and the monophysites. The Chalcedon faction in the East and almost all of the western churches insisted on the hypostatic union of two natures and two wills.

Monophysitism and monothelitism remain beliefs of a number of Christian communities, especially the Armenian Orthodox and Coptic Christians.

<u>Key Points</u>

- The place of the Law in the scheme of salvation was still an issue for some into the fifth century.

- The person of Jesus still confused large numbers of theologians. There was a great number of opinions across several possible combinations of natures and wills.
- The permutations of theological speculation on the person of Jesus are actually much more complicated than presented above. Many theories have been passed over.

The Triumph of the Orthodox Catholics

The First Evidence

The term proto-catholic or proto-orthodox suggests a nurturing beginning to catholicism or orthodoxy which was sufficiently different from catholicism or orthodoxy as to require a distinction. This, indeed, is the case. Not the Roman Catholic Church, not any of the Eastern Orthodox Churches, not the Anglican Church, not any other church is nearly identical to the first Christians in Palestine or to the proto-catholic congregations which blossomed with the third generation of Christians, in spite of claims and protests to the contrary. The proto-catholics had no theology as such, only an enthusiastic belief in the resurrection of Jesus and an acute anticipation of his second coming in glory. They had only nascent and incompatible, from congregation to congregation, Christologies. They had no canon of scripture outside of the Hebrew Bible, no creeds as the word is used today, no standardized cults, no central authority coordinating congregations. These things developed over time, but they did not spring wholly developed out of the head of James, Peter, Paul, or anyone else. They did not exist almost anywhere through most of the first five centuries.

The very first written expression of proto-catholicism is the previously mentioned first Epistle of Clement. In sum, it states that

1. The apostles received a gospel from Jesus;
2. Jesus was commissioned by God;
3. The received gospel was validated by the resurrection of Jesus and the testimony (?) of the Holy Ghost;

4. The apostles went forth to preach to the world;
5. When the apostles left a mission place, they appointed bishops and deacons to minister to the congregation;
6. Bishops and deacons were appointed from very ancient times.

Statements two and three may be granted, but every other proposition is arguable. The first proposition is the most vital. What gospel did the Apostles receive, the hidden knowledge claimed by the Gnostic Christians? There has been no claim of a hidden gospel. Yet, one can read the surviving gospels many times and still not know, specifically, the nature of the person of Jesus or the nature of God. This is an historical fact established by the extremely wide variety of opinions which are sincerely held. (There are about twenty thousand denominations and independent Christian churches in the world today.) Any other proposition is a matter of opinion.

The gospels were redacted many years after the ministry of Jesus. There is ample evidence of multiple redactors and multiple theologies. The gospels we can read today do not categorically define the person of Jesus, the essence of the deity, or many other of the dogmas so cherished by the Catholics and Orthodox. While many dogmas could be cited as examples, the "mother of God" controversy started by the Catholic Patriarch of Constantinople, Nestorius, serves as an example of speculative theology pile-driven into the gospels on the basis of the slim reed of "teaching authority." This is an historical fact. Any other proposition is a matter of opinion.

This leads directly to the proto-catholic/orthodox claims that they alone could define true doctrine (orthodoxy), the so called "teaching authority." While this is not claimed directly in Clement's letter, it is suggested in his sixth proposition: bishops and deacons were appointed from ancient times. The implicit argument here is that the bishops are successors to the Apostles, who received a gospel from Jesus on the authority of God. There is no evidence of an appointed bishop anywhere in the first centuries of Christianity. There is evidence of the use of lot in *Acts* to select a successor to Judas, and there are many evidences of elections. Where are the appointments? In any case, the transmission of teaching authority requires explanation as to exactly what is the ontological nature of that authority and exactly how it is transmitted. The claim to a teaching authority on the basis of the canonical gospels has been demolished by history, including, obviously, the sin and error in the church. Any other proposition is a matter of opinion.

The nature of the office of bishop is obscure in the earliest scriptures and in the *Teaching*. The word is used as synonymous with presbyter and deacon in many places in the New Testament and beyond. Challenge: show how and when the distinct offices operated.

When, a century or so later, Irenaeus claims that he knows Gnosticism is false because no bishop has ever embraced Gnosticism, his argument falls on its face when the Patriarchs of Antioch, Alexandria, Constantinople and Rome, omitting many, many other bishops, are declared anathema or otherwise disciplined. These are the four most important Patriarchates in the world (after Rome had been elevated to the status of Alexandria by the Nicene Council), and they have been condemned by the opinion of many Christian churches. The notion of infallibility of bishops has been demolished by history. Any other proposition is a matter of opinion.

It is an historical fact that the developing Catholic/Orthodox Church, like other religions, served as the handmaiden of the government, in this case, the Emperor. It was the Emperor who convoked ecumenical and some lower ranked councils of bishops. It was the Emperor or his legate who presided at these councils, and the decisions of the councils always and everywhere depended upon the favor (grace) of the Emperor. The petitions of the Catholic/Orthodox and Arian churches to the Emperor clearly establish his authority over church doctrine. Orthodox theology served political expediency, and orthodoxy, as in the case of Constantine and Arianism, was politically expedient.

The fourth proposition in the summary of Clement's letter, that the Apostles went forth to preach to the world, is legend, not historical fact. However, this legend was used by some orthodox Christians to exterminate aborigines in the new world. Since the gospels charged the Apostles to preach to the whole world and since they believed that the gospels were the inerrant word of God, and since these aborigines had not been evangelized, it follows that these aborigines were not human.

They are sub-human animals, perhaps unfit to eat but not unfit to kill, especially if they had something European Christians wanted.

Key Points

- The Catholic/Orthodox view maintains that there has been an unbroken succession of bishops from the apostolic age to the present day. This claim is disputed by many who see the gradual development of church offices starting seriously, but haltingly, with the third generation of Christians. The letters of Ignatius of Antioch, written about ten years after Clement's epistle, show the continuing development of church offices, raising questions about his and others' understanding of the office.

- The Catholic/Orthodox view maintains that heresy was always a choice, a deliberate deviation from orthodox doctrine. This view is manifestly unhistorical inasmuch as orthodox doctrine developed over centuries in response and opposition to Gnostic theologies. Furthermore, that viewpoint does not take into account honest differences of conscience and is at least uncharitable. One should not be exiled, be tortured, or be killed because one believes that Mary is not the mother of God.

- The Catholic/Orthodox view maintains that it alone held the keys to the doctrinal truth of Christianity received directly from Christ. Any perusal of the surviving gospels establishes beyond a doubt that many interpretations of doctrine can be harvested from these works, and that the gospels contain no consensus rule of faith to assess orthodoxy. This proposition is manifested in the several centuries required to develop a reasonably complete, but still incomplete, body of orthodox doctrines (although one must wonder at how much further orthodoxy can read the gospels to find dogmas beyond the infallibility of the Pope or the bodily assumption of

Mary). At least one bishop of the Patriarchates at Rome, Alexandria, Antioch and Constantinople has been condemned, along with countless other bishops. The office of bishop, or even pope, as a matter of historical fact has not guaranteed orthodoxy or the absence of sin and error.

- The Catholic/Orthodox view maintains that from the beginning the Roman Church had primacy and dominion over all catholic churches, a proposition denied by a large number of catholic churches, both East and West, Latin and Greek.

- The first Christian churches, the congregations in Palestine, very likely founded by the Apostles of Jesus, espoused a variety of now heterodox views and paid no attention whatsoever to the Roman Church.

- In antiquity and even later, the Catholic/Orthodox Churches were subservient to the Emperor. When the Western Empire dissolved, the Roman Catholic Church arrogated to itself the Emperor's role of head of the Christian Church and became a temporal authority as well, first by its *de facto* presence, then through the fabrication in the 8th century of *Constantine's Donation*, a document which purports to give to the Bishop of Rome lands, the trappings of monarchy, and suzerainty over all bishops and all church matters, as if Constantine could give what, apparently, God had not given.

From Congregation to Church

The individual proto-catholic congregations made efforts to communicate with one another, largely because they felt they were part of the same mission—commanded by Jesus himself—to evangelize the world. Each of them had a local history, many had local martyrs. As they reflected upon their histories, they realized they had something of value to pass on to the next generation. Their histories should not be lost, and their martyrs, confessors, and other heroes must be remembered.

Two other areas of concern included the interference of the Judaizers and the preaching of the Gnostics. Individual congregations communicated to find out how other congregations were handling these issues. They needed mutual support and good ideas to reinforce true doctrine and oppose false doctrine.

As the first generation of Christians was passing on without having been taken up in the Rapture, the second generation of Christians began thinking of these concerns more seriously: there could possibly be another generation (the third, perhaps a fourth?) of Christians. Certainly, the third generation, without having to listen in detail to the first generation, took these issues very, very seriously and resolved to form permanent governments.

There had always, of course, been some form of leadership, like the "pillars" of the Jerusalem congregation. Now, however, governance needed to become more formal, with someone clearly in charge, a monarch—by far the most common form of government—supported by lower ranking officials. Thus, in the late first century and continuing well into the second century, we see the development of church offices. Into the second century, the offices are not clearly defined: *episcopos* (meaning overseer, then bishop), *presbyteros* (meaning elder, then priest), and *diakonos* (meaning server, then deacon as a church office) were often used interchangeably by the proto-catholic congregations which were building these governments. It took time to separate the office of bishop and priest and to assign duties to each and to the deacons. Also, any city of decent size had several congregations with several overseers/bishops. Jurisdictional issues had to be solved. When congregations sorted out these things, they became churches.

Key Point

- Government became necessary for congregations because of the need to transmit history and tradition, to distinguish between orthodox and heterodox beliefs, and, most surely, to address the eschatological problem, the failure of Jesus to return.

The Triumph

The Gnostics helped the orthodox to succeed by their elitist orientation and bearing. According to the Gnostics, only a few people are clever enough to benefit from Gnosticism. Unlike the proto-catholics, they did not recruit wholesale numbers of people, only the few, the most intelligent, and so forth. The characteristic Gnostic attitude of abhorring the flesh (as well as all other material) led these congregations to despise the flesh and adopt measures to punish it. Year round asceticism does not often draw large crowds.

On the other hand, the proto-catholics believed they had a mission to convert the whole world. While they exhibited some tendency toward asceticism, this tendency proved to be relatively moderate. In their partial acceptance of the Hebrew Bible, they assumed the mantle of an ancient religion. In rejecting observance of the Law, they unloaded the biggest obstacle to potential converts.

The non-Gnostic congregations in Palestine tended to dispute among themselves regarding the degree to which Christians should observe the Law. Their general refusal to support the uprising of 66-73 against Roman occupation caused them to lose support in the synagogues. After the destruction of the Temple (70) and the defeat at Masada (73), the Jewish attitude toward sectarian Christians hardened until they were branded as heretics and expelled from the synagogues in the period around 80-90. At this point, these Christians had either to revert to Judaism or to a Pauline form of Christianity, a difficult decision for those who regarded Paul as the arch-heresiarch. Those which could do neither carried on until the third and fourth centuries. Some Pauline congregations already disputed the teachings of some Palestinian congregations, and, some Palestinian congregations were stigmatized as heretics. The point is, the first Christian congregations, those in Palestine, founded, almost certainly, by the Apostles, died out. Those which survived for a while would have been anathema to the proto-catholic churches.

That leaves the proto-catholic congregations founded by Paul and such other Apostles as actually travelled outside Palestine and their companions. There is no need to repeat the slim assurances offered by these congregations as to their claim to be the one, true form of Christianity and the objections thereto. How, then, did the Roman Catholic Church in the West come to dominate the Christian religion for many centuries?

Location, location, location, seems to be the answer. Being in the right place at the right time is an often cited key to success, and that can explain the rising dominance of the Roman Church.

The seat of the Empire was Rome. The Empire had a view of Christianity by observing the Christians "down the street." When it became desirable for some reason, or necessary for other reasons, to communicate with Christians, either informally, or later, officially, the government would certainly have communicated with the Roman Church, not a provincial church. Nothing official, of course, even though Nerva had recognized Christianity as a religion different from Judaism. This alone would give the Roman Church the primacy of honor which many, if not most, if not all Christian Churches were willing to cede to the Roman Church. But Rome did even more: it provided a governance model, the monarchic bishop. This made people at the top of the other churches feel more comfortable and more disposed to grant primacy of honor.

With the toleration of Christianity under Constantine in the early fourth century, the Roman Church becomes an official source of information for the Emperor. He makes the final decisions on church discipline and doctrine, but he is guided by the advice he receives from the Roman Church. He doesn't really care about religion as such: he cares about stability and order.

When Christianity is declared to be the state religion toward the end of the fourth century, the Roman Church furnished the Emperor with lists of troublemakers, so that he could take appropriate measures to secure the peace and tranquility of the Empire through homicides, tortures, banishments, expropriations of property, and so forth. The Spanish Inquisition merely reenacted the good old days. In its defense, the Empire merely reenacted the good old days, for thus it had ever been, religion as handmaiden of the Ruler. Christianity has not been different from polytheism in this respect.

Key Points

- The competition to the proto-catholics proved to be insubstantial. The elitist Gnostics, whose theologies propelled the development of Catholic theologies, and whose canon of scripture forced the development of our canon of scripture, would never become a mass movement. Although Gnosticism exists to this day, it does not compete vigorously with mainline religions.

- Also insubstantial were the original Christians, the members of the Palestinian congregations founded by the Apostles. Having no means or time to develop their theologies and church government before their fatal expulsion from the synagogues, with few exceptions they disappeared into Judaism or Greek Christianity. Such was the fruit of the Apostles.

- The Roman Church followed the Roman government in form, attempting, insofar as possible to institute a monarchical ruler/overseer/bishop. This took some time but eventually succeeded.

- Whatever the form of its governance, the Roman Church supplied the Emperor with the Emperor's understanding of Christianity.

- As the Empire grew more tolerant of Christianity and eventually established it as the state religion, the power of the Roman Church increased, such that among the Christian Churches, it would become able to centralize power, to effect its doctrinal predilections and more or less to define orthodoxy, until 1054, when Eastern Orthodox Churches severed their connections with Rome over doctrinal disputes which most of us cannot comprehend.

Chapter Nine: A Very Brief Look at Documentary Sources in Genesis

The Documents behind the Pentateuch

Jean Astruc constructed a theory of pre-existing documents which, he theorized, Moses had sewed together to come up with the Pentateuch, also known, for over one thousand years, as the five Books of Moses. The fact that Moses could not be the author or redactor of the Pentateuch does not diminish Astruc's genius in proposing the documentary theory behind the Pentateuch. Modern scholars have developed his work and discern four underlying documents, plus some ancient poetry, and, of course, the occasional hands of redactors.

The oldest source may date from the time of the monarchy, although many scholars date it several hundred years later. This source uses the personal name Yahweh as its term for the deity. For this reason the source is usually called J, the initial letter in the German language for the name Yahweh.

The Yahwist source is one of two narrative strands. The other narrative source, the Elohist is referred to as E. E uses the term Elohim, the Hebrew generic term for God, plural in number, when referring to the deity. In English translations, Yahweh is usually rendered "Lord" and Elohim as "God."

The third source is designated P for Priestly. While the priestly cast goes back centuries to the earliest historical age of Israel, the P source may be the newest of the four principal sources. P generally reports facts, figures, and genealogy. It reports in a matter of fact style and generally lacks human qualities. P's God is very remote. It uses the terms Elohim or El Shaddai when referring to the deity.

The fourth source is called D, for Deuteronomy, because it is found more or less exclusively in that book. The style of this book distinguishes it from the four other books of the Pentateuch.

The sources are identified by scholars principally on the basis of subject matter, vocabulary, syntax and style. There is some disagreement among scholars regarding particular passages, since the criteria are somewhat subjective. The style of writing in Deuteronomy is judged to be one of a kind, and J and E are narrative strands, while P is generally not. Clearly, there is room to disagree on the application of principles to specific passages.

In addition to the principle sources, there are remnants of very old poetry, and, very likely, several redactors.

Three Illustrations

Two accounts of the Creation of the World

The oldest non-fragment texts of biblical writings are called unicals. These texts are written in Greek upper case letters without punctuation or paragraphing. Our translations are divided into chapters and verses (as well as paragraphs) which divisions date from the middle ages. We are about to explore one instance where the miss-assignment of verses has affected the interpretation of the text for many English speaking Christians, but perhaps not for you. If you use the English Standard Version, or the King James translation, or one of several others which rely on the same family of texts, you will not see verse four of chapter two split into two parts, 4a and 4b.

The first two chapters of the Book of Genesis contain two accounts of the creation of the world. The first account begins at Genesis 1: 1 and ends at Genesis 2: 4a. The second begins at Genesis 2: 4b and continues to the end of the chapter two. In the consensus of scholars, the first account derives from the P source, the second from the J source. The texts are reproduced for convenience.

"In the beginning, God created the heavens and the earth. The earth was without form and void, and darkness was over the face of the deep. And the Spirit of God was hovering over the face of the waters.

"And God said, 'Let there be light,' and there was light. And God saw that the light was good. And God separated the light from the darkness. God called the light Day, and the darkness he called Night. And there was evening and there was morning, the first day.

"And God said, 'Let there be an expanse in the midst of the waters, and let it separate the waters from the waters.' And God made the expanse and separated the waters that were under the expanse from the waters that were above the expanse. And it was so. And God called the expanse Heaven. And there was evening and there was morning, the second day.

"And God said, 'Let the waters under the heavens be gathered together into one place, and let dry land appear.' And it was so. God called the dry land Earth, and the waters that were gathered together he called Seas. And God saw that it was good.

"And God said, 'Let the earth sprout vegetation, plants yielding seed, and fruit trees bearing fruit in which is their seed, each according to its kind, on the earth.' And it was so. The earth brought forth vegetation, plants yielding seed according to their own kinds, and trees bearing fruit in which is their seed, each according to its kind. And God saw that it was good. And there was evening and there was morning, the third day.

"And God said, 'Let there be lights in the expanse of the heavens to separate the day from the night. And let them be for signs and seasons, and for days and years, and let them be lights in the expanse of the heavens to give light upon the earth.' And it was so. And God made the two great lights—the greater light to rule the day and the lesser light to rule the night—and the stars. And God set them in the expanse of the heavens to give light on the earth to rule over the day and over the night, and to separate the light from the darkness. And God saw that it was good. And there was evening and there was morning, the fourth day.

"And God said, 'Let the waters swarm with swarms of living creatures, and let birds fly above the earth across the expanse of the heavens.' So God created the great sea creatures and every living creature that moves, with which the waters swarm, according to their kinds, and every winged bird according to its kind. And God saw that it was good. And God blessed them, saying, 'Be fruitful and multiply and fill the waters in the seas, and let birds multiply on the earth.' And there was evening and there was morning, the fifth day.

"And God said, 'Let the earth bring forth living creatures according to their kinds—livestock and creeping things and beasts of the earth according to their kinds.' And it was so. And God made the beasts of the earth according to their kinds and the livestock according to their kinds, and everything that creeps on the ground according to its kind. And God saw that it was good.

"Then God said, 'Let us make man in our image, after our likeness. And let them have dominion over the fish of the sea and over the birds of the heavens and over the livestock and over all the earth and over every creeping thing that creeps on the earth.'

"So God created man in his own image,
In the image of God he created him;
Male and female he created them.

"And God blessed them. And God said to them, 'Be fruitful and multiply and fill the earth and subdue it, and have dominion over the fish of the sea and over the birds of the heavens and over every living thing that moves on the earth.' And God said, 'Behold, I have given you every plant yielding seed that is on the face of the earth, and every tree with seed in its fruit. You shall have them for food. And to every beast of the earth and to every bird of the heavens and to everything that creeps on the earth, everything that has the breath of life, I have given every green plant for food.' And it was so. And God saw everything that he had made, and behold, it was very good. And there was evening and there was morning, the sixth day.

"Thus the heavens and the earth were finished, and all the host of them. And on the seventh day God finished his work that he had done, and he rested on the seventh day from all his work that he had done. So God blessed the seventh day and made it holy, because on it God rested from all his work that he had done in creation. [Such is the story of the creation of the heavens and the earth.][66]

---

66 The English Standard Version, based on its selection of original texts, differs in

"These are the generations
of the heavens and the earth when they were created,
in the day that the Lord God made the earth and the
heavens." (Genesis 1: 1 - 2: 4)

"[When the Lord God made the earth and the heavens—] when
no bush in the field was yet in the land and no small plant of the field
had yet sprung up—for the Lord God had not caused it to rain on the
land, and there was no man to work the ground, and a mist was going
up from the land and was watering the whole face of the ground—then
the Lord God formed the man of dust from the ground and breathed
into his nostrils the breath of life, and the man became a living creature.
And the Lord God planted a garden in Eden, in the east, and there he
put the man whom he had formed. And out of the ground the Lord
God made to spring up every tree that is pleasant to the sight and good
for food. The tree of life was in the midst of the garden, and the tree of
the knowledge of good and evil.

"A river flowed out of Eden to water the garden, and there it divided
and became four rivers. The name of the first is the Pishon. It is the one
that flowed around the whole land of Havilah, where there is gold. And
the gold of that land is good; bdellium and onyx stone are there. The
name of the second river is the Gihon. It is the one that flowed around
the whole land of Cush. And the name of the third river is the Tigris,
which flows east of Assyria. And the fourth river is the Euphrates.

"The Lord God took the man and put him in the garden of Eden to
work it and keep it. And the Lord God commanded the man, saying,
'You may surely eat of every tree of the garden, but of the tree of the
knowledge of good and evil you shall not eat, for in the day that you eat
of it you shall surely die.'

"Then the Lord God said, 'It is not good that the man should be
alone; I will make him a helper fit for him.' Now out of the ground the

---

verse four of chapter two from many other translations. A more typical rendering
of an older text might be: "Such is the story of the creation of the heavens and the
earth." (verse 4a), followed by a new sentence: "When the Lord God made the
earth and the heavens—"(verse 4b). These elements are combined in the rendering
quoted above, but at a loss of discrimination between the sources of the texts and,
indeed, a common understanding to the texts.

Lord God had formed every beast of the field and every bird of the heavens and brought them to the man to see what he would call them. And whatever the man called every living creature, that was its name. The man gave names to all livestock and to the birds of the heavens and to every beast of the field. But for Adam there was not found a helper fit for him. So the Lord God caused a deep sleep to fall upon the man, and while he slept took one of his ribs and closed up its place with flesh. And the rib that the Lord God had taken from the man he made into a woman and brought her to the man. Then the man said,

> 'This at last is bone of my bones
>> and flesh of my flesh;
> She shall be called woman,
>> because she was taken out of Man.'

"Therefore a man shall leave his father and his mother and hold fast to his wife, and they shall become one flesh. And the man and his wife were both naked and were not ashamed." (Genesis 2: 4b – 25)

When most people speak of the biblical account of the creation of the world, they do not distinguish between the two accounts, in part because their translations are based on Greek texts which treat verse four of chapter two differently. Yet, the two accounts are remarkably different regardless of the translation of verse four.

The personal name of a particular god, Yahweh (translated as Lord), marks vividly the beginning of a new source. Man is the center of the J account. It even begins differently from the P account. The making of earth and heaven exhibits the anthropocentric, earthy orientation of J, while the creation of heaven and earth, the P account, keep man at a distance in the cosmos, a player, an ornament on the stage of the universe. God has the speaking part in the P account, but man has the speaking part in the J account.

What may next be most evident is the contrast in style between the two accounts. The first account sounds like a script to be recited. It displays the cosmos as a marvelous masterpiece of the creator: man is simply a small part of the work. There is very little human emotion. Indeed, humans are simply another product of God, created on the same day as the animals.

In the second account, man is the center of the story. Yahweh forms man from the dust of earth and personally breathes the breath of life into his nostrils before there was rain for vegetation. Yahweh plants a garden for man, and forms beasts and birds for his use and companionship. Yahweh brings the beasts to man to name them. When Yahweh understands that these are not sufficient to relieve man's loneliness, Yahweh creates woman with the tenderness of forming woman from the man rather than from the earth. This is nothing at all like the first account, and cannot be reconciled to it without violence to the texts.

It should be noted that the P account reflects the Babylonian creation epic, *Enuma Elish* in several different ways, including the telltale marker of the order in which events are elaborated. Order is an important criterion in adjudging dependence.

Two Married Accounts Intertwined

The story of Joseph, which occupies a good deal of the latter part of Genesis, illustrates how a redactor joined together two accounts, E and J, into a single narrative. This occurs several times in the stories about Joseph, but we will confine ourselves to one short section telling the tale of his being sold into slavery in Egypt. (Genesis 37: 2b–36)

The opening verses set the stage for the ensuing drama, drama being a reliable sign of J. Israel, the name used by J for Jacob, manifests his special affection for Joseph by giving him an ornamented tunic. His brothers resent Joseph for his father's special love.

Joseph makes matters worse by telling them about two dreams which they interpret as suggesting Joseph would have dominion over them. When he recounts the second dream to his father, Israel, Israel demonstrates a similar reaction.

Israel sends Joseph to find out how his brothers and their flocks are doing. As he approaches them, they plot to kill him. (J, Genesis 37: 2b-20)

At this point, the E account comes in. Reuben urges his brothers to avoid bloodshed by tossing Joseph into a dry cistern, presumably to die. Actually, Reuben intended to come back and rescue Joseph. (E, vv.

21-24) In E, Reuben is Joseph's protector, and the name of their father is Jacob, not Israel.

Back to J. While supping, the brothers see a caravan of Ishmaelites, and Judah proposes selling Joseph to them, thus avoiding having to kill their own brother. (J, vv. 25-27) Judah is Joseph's protector in J, and it is to the Ishmaelites that they sell Joseph.

Meanwhile, Midianite traders pass by and they pull Joseph out of the pit. (E, verse 28a)

The brothers sell Joseph to the Ishmaelites for twenty pieces of silver. (J, verse 28 b)

Joseph is taken to Egypt by the Midianites. (E, verse 28c)

E continues for the remainder of the story: Reuben's horrible discovery that Joseph is missing, the plot by the brothers to soak his tunic in blood so as to suggest an animal killed him, Jacob's sorrow over Joseph's apparent death, and the final verse telling of the sale by the Midianites of Joseph to Patiphar.

Why intertwine two separate accounts? Since the event could not have happened two times, the two accounts must be reconciled into one.

Why not just skip one account? Which one does one skip? It is clear that the redactor(s) held both accounts in high esteem, needing to be preserved, in some sense sacred.

Another Source

In addition to the interventions of the redactors, there are occasional other sources for Genesis. The longest coherent passage may be the so-called Blessings of Jacob (Genesis 49: 2-27). Here is a two verse sample to explain the "so called" of the previous sentence.

> "'Reuben, you are my firstborn,
>> my might, and the first fruits of my strength,
>> preeminent in dignity and preeminent in power.
> Unstable as water, you shall not have preeminence,
>> because you went up to your father's bed;
>> then you defiled it—he went up to my couch!'" (49: 3-4)

This is followed by a curse in verse seven. Thus, the blessing devolves into a curse.

The entire poem is thought to be an antique poem, deriving, possibly, from the days before the monarchy, well before the other sources were developed.

Key Points

- There are at least six sources identified by scholars as sources for the Pentateuch.
- J, one of two narrative sources, uses the personal name of the particular god Yahweh when speaking of the deity. This source names the successor of Isaac Israel, not Jacob, but otherwise employs no special vocabulary. J is anthropocentric, interested in human beings and human feelings. Its style is dramatic and forceful. Events speak for themselves.
- E, the second narrative source, usually explains what is going on rather than letting the actions in the narrative constitute the message. Man is not the center of its attention, but Elohim, a generic word, plural in form, for God. Man in E is distant from God, who speaks to man through intermediaries such as angels and dreams.
- A third source, P, is concerned mostly about genealogy, maintaining legitimate contact with the past. Man is very remote from God, who is named either Elohim or El Shaddai. Its style is matter of fact, bordering on the boring.
- The fourth source is called D, for Deuteronomy, because it is found more or less exclusively, with respect to the Pentateuch, in that book. The style of this book distinguishes it from the four other books of the Pentateuch.
- In addition to the four documentary sources above, there are remnants of very old poetry, and, very likely, several redactors.

Afterword

Descriptive Approaches to the Study of Sacred Scripture

Here are four (among many) different ways of looking at sacred scripture. Most of us start with the first: we are creatures of the culture which bred us. The last describes faith, faith which is necessary to accept a triune God and Jesus Christ as God-Man. The second describes the scientific method, and the third describes polemicists, people who maintain that their (version of the) truth is the only truth.

> We are children of our culture. Little children. We live in its embrace: we dance on its floor, marvel at its ceiling, and respect its walls. We do not think about it. We are rarely conscious of its most fundamental beliefs. We recite its creeds as mantras and sing its anthems without reflecting on the words. To question is to defect. Why would we leave the clan, the church, the country? It's so inconvenient.

> "Plurality should not be posited without necessity."[67] Occam's (Ockham's) razor. A more typical, but less accurate rendition is, "The simplest solution is usually the best solution."

> "Seek and you will find."[68] No truer description can be written of a theologian before an open bible.

> "The Son of God was crucified; I am not ashamed even though I am required to be ashamed of it.

---

67 Skeptic's Dictionary (on-line resource).
68 Matthew 7: 7.

And the Son of God died; it is by all means believable, because it is silly.

And He was buried, and rose up from the dead; the fact is certain, because it is impossible."[69]

---

69   Tertullian; *On the Flesh of Christ*, 5: 4.

Sources

We have added no new ideas to the remarkable findings presented within. All of the new ideas come from very highly respected biblical scholars. We are simply journalists collecting credible ideas for your consideration.

There follows a list of the most important sources for this work. All of them are important, but we add the designations "very important" and "very, very important" to those we believe contribute most to our discussion. Also, we suggest that each source is "very accessible," "accessible," or "difficult" in terms of our conception of the ability of ordinary people for whom scripture study is an occasional pursuit to comprehend the several presentations. These recommendations on importance and accessibility are simple value judgments and may differ from the value judgments of others. We urge you to read them all for a fuller understanding of these serious topics.

Bauer, Walter. *Orthodoxy and Heresy in Earliest Christianity*. (Fortress Press; Philadelphia, 1971.) Very, very important. Difficult.

Brown, Raymond E. Introduction to *The Gospel according to John I-XII*, *The Anchor Bible, v. 29*. (Doubleday and Company, Inc., Garden City, New York, 1966.) Very important. Accessible.

Bultmann, Rudolf. *Primitive Christianity in its Contemporary Setting*. (Meridian Books; New York, 1964.) Accessible.

Bultmann, Rudolf. *Faith and Understanding*. (Fortress Press; Philadelphia, 1987.) Accessible.

Conzelman, Hans. *An Outline of the Theology of the New Testament*. (Harper & Row; New York, 1969.) Accessible.

Cozens, M. L. *A Handbook of Heresies* (abridged edition). (Sheed and Ward; New York, undated.) Very accessible.

Crossan, John Dominic. *The Historical Jesus: The Life of a Mediterranean Jewish Peasant.* (Harper Collins; New York, 1992.) Very important. Accessible.

Crossan, John Dominic. *The Essential Jesus: Original Sayings and Earliest Images.* (Harper; San Francisco, 1984.) Very important. Difficult.

Crossan, John Dominic. *The Birth of Christianity.* (Harper Collins; San Francisco, 1998.) Very, very important. Accessible.

Cullman, Oscar. *Baptism in the New Testament.* (Westminster Press; Philadelphia, 1950.) Accessible.

Cullman, Oscar. *The Christology of the NT.* Revised edition translated by Guthrie and Hael. (Westminster Press; Philadelphia, 1963.) Very important. Accessible.

Cullman, Oscar. *Early Christian Worship.* (Westminster Press; Philadelphia, 1953.) . Accessible.

Cullman, Oscar. *The New Testament: an Introduction for the General Reader.* (Westminster Press; 1968, Philadelphia.) Very important. Accessible.

Davies, J. G. *The Early Christian Church.* (Henry Holt & Co.; 1965, NY.) Accessible.

Dewey, Arthur J. and Miller, Robert J. *The Complete Gospel Parallels.* (Polebridge Press; Salem, OR, 2012.) Accessible.

Ehrman, Bart D. *Misquoting Jesus.* (Harper; San Francisco, 2005.) Very accessible.

Ehrman, Bart D. *Lost Christianities*. (Oxford University Press; New York, 2003.) Very important. Very accessible.

Eusebius. (Translated by G. A. Williamson) *The History of the Church from Christ to Constantine*. (Dorset Press; 1984.) Accessible.

Finklestein, Israel and Silberman, Neil Asher. *The Bible Unearthed*. (The Free Press; New York, 2002). Very, very important. Very accessible.

Gimbutas, Marija. *The Living Goddesses*. (University of California Press, 2001.) Accessible.

Jeremias, Joachim. *Rediscovering the Parables*. (Charles Scribner's Sons; 1966, New York.) Accessible.

Jeremias, Joachim. *The Prayers of Jesus*. (Fortress Press; Philadelphia, 1966.) Accessible.

Jeremias, Joachim. *The Eucharistic Words of Jesus*. (Fortress Press; Philadelphia, 1966.) Very important. Accessible.

Lightfoot, J. B. and Harmer, J. R. *The Apostolic Fathers*. (Baker Book House; Grand Rapids, MI, 1988.) Accessible.

Pagels, Elaine. *The Gnostic Gospels*. (Random House; New York, 1979.) Very important. Accessible.

Reinach, Solomon. *Orpheus*. (Horace Liveright; NY, 1930.) Very important. Accessible.

Sanders, E. P., and Davies, Margaret. *Studying the Synoptic Problem*. (Trinity Press International; Philadelphia, 1989.) Accessible.

Schiffman, Lawrence H. *From Text to Tradition*. (Ktav Publishing House; Hoboken, NJ, 1991.) Accessible.

Speiser, E. A. *Genesis. The Anchor Bible.* (Doubleday & Co.; Garden City, NY, 1986.) Very important. Accessible.

<u>Additional Resources</u>

Encyclopedia Britannica (15th edition, 1995) articles:

Asceticism
Ancient Mid-East Religions
Biblical Literature
Christianity
Greek and Roman Civilization
Judaism
Mystery Religions
Religious and Spiritual Belief, Systems of
Palestine
Many smaller articles on particular people, church offices, and sects. Accessible.

The Bible's Buried Secrets: <u>http://www.pbs.org/wgbh/nova/ancient/bibles-buried-secrets.html</u> <u>and related articles</u>. Very, very important. Very accessible. Transcript only is now available on the website, along with supporting essays, but the program may be purchased on disk. Buy the disk.

<u>http://www. Earlychristianwritings.com</u> and related articles. Very, very important. Accessible.

<u>http://www.Gnosis.org</u>. and related articles. Very important. Accessible.